Excel Basic Skills

Spelling, Vocabulary, Grammar and Punctuation

1–2 Years

Ages 6–8

Get the Results You Want!

Peter Clutterbuck

© 1998 Peter Clutterbuck and Pascal Press
Reprinted 2000, 2001, 2002, 2003, 2004, 2006, 2007 (twice), 2008 (twice), 2009, 2010, 2012, 2013, 2014, 2016 (twice), 2017, 2019, 2020 (twice), 2021 (twice), 2023

ISBN 978 1 86441 341 0

Pascal Press
PO Box 250
Glebe NSW 2037
(02) 9198 1748
www.pascalpress.com.au

Publisher: Vivienne Joannou
Text design and typesetting by Tamie Lowson
Cover by DiZign Pty Ltd
Printed by Vivar Printing/Green Giant Press

Reproduction and communication for educational purposes
The Australian Copyright Act 1968 (the Act) allows a maximum of one chapter or 10% of the pages of this work, whichever is the greater, to be reproduced and/or communicated by any educational institution for its educational purposes provided that the educational institution (or the body that administers it) has given a remuneration notice to Copyright Agency under the Act.

For details of the Copyright Agency licence for educational institutions contact:

Copyright Agency
Level 12, 66 Goulburn Street
Sydney NSW 2000
Telephone: (02) 9394 7600
Facsimile: (02) 9394 7601
E-mail: memberservices@copyright.com.au

Reproduction and communication for other purposes
Except as permitted under the Act (for example, a fair dealing for the purposes of study, research, criticism or review) no part of this book may be reproduced, stored in a retrieval system, communicated or transmitted in any form or by any means without prior written permission. All inquiries should be made to the publisher at the address above.

Contents

Spelling and Vocabulary Years 1 and 2

About this book 4

Year 1

Spelling

Unit 1 Adding Initial Letters 5
Unit 2 Changing Final Letters 6
Unit 3 Adding Vowels 7
Unit 4 Initial Blends 8
Unit 5 Final Blends 9
Unit 6 Double Letters (Consonants) 10
Unit 7 Double Letters (Vowels) 11
Unit 8 Sight Words 12
Unit 9 Word Building (1) 13
Unit 10 Word Building (2) 14
Unit 11 Word Shapes 15
Unit 12 Words that Sound the Same 16
Unit 13 Sounds 17
Unit 14 Letter Patterns 18
Unit 15 Joining Word Pieces 19
Unit 16 Jumbled Words 20
Unit 17 Plural Words 21

Vocabulary

Unit 18 Words for Pictures 22
Unit 19 Compound Words 23
Unit 20 Opposites 24
Unit 21 Homophones 25
Unit 22 Anagrams 26
Unit 23 Words with the Same Meaning 27
Unit 24 Dropping Letters 28
Unit 25 Word Meanings 29

Year 2

Spelling

Unit 26 Initial Blends 30
Unit 27 Final Blends 31
Unit 28 Sounds 32
Unit 29 Word Building 33
Unit 30 Problem Words 34
Unit 31 Letter Patterns 35
Unit 32 Identifying Words 36
Answers (lift-out section) A1–A4
Unit 33 Double Letters 37
Unit 34 Base Words 38
Unit 35 Small Words 39
Unit 36 Adding Letters 40
Unit 37 Letter Pieces 41
Unit 38 Syllables 42
Unit 39 Silent Letters 43
Unit 40 Plural Words 44
Unit 41 Spelling Rules (1) 45
Unit 42 Spelling Rules (2) 46

Vocabulary

Unit 43 Compound Words 47
Unit 44 Opposites 48
Unit 45 Homophones 49
Unit 46 Anagrams 50
Unit 47 Words with the Same Meaning 51
Unit 48 Word Meanings 52
Unit 49 Word Families 53
Unit 50 Similes 54

Grammar and Punctuation Years 1 and 2

Grammar

Unit 51 Using *a* or *an* before Words 55
Unit 52 Nouns (1) 56
Unit 53 Nouns (2) 57
Unit 54 Verbs 58
Unit 55 Verb Tense 59
Unit 56 Verbs—*is*/*are*, *was*/*were* 60
Unit 57 Adjectives 61
Unit 58 Adverbs 62
Unit 59 Prepositions 63
Unit 60 Pronouns 64
Unit 61 Conjunctions 65
Unit 62 Phrases 66
Unit 63 Sentences 67

Punctuation

Unit 64 Statements 68
Unit 65 Questions 69
Unit 66 Statements and Questions 70
Unit 67 Statements, Questions and Exclamations 71
Unit 68 Commas 72

About this book

The activities in this book have been designed to help lower primary students improve their basic language skills and introduce them to the important elements that make up the structure of our language.

Parents and teachers are well aware that the skills of spelling, grammar, vocabulary and punctuation are vital for children to confidently master language development throughout their primary school years. Although at this age level children should not be bombarded with the complexities of such things as grammatical constructions and specific terminology, it is important they are made aware that there are a variety of devices used to ensure clarity and correctness in both writing and speaking. The activities in this book will provide a solid foundation of language knowledge which children of this age group will carry throughout later primary and secondary years of schooling.

The activities in this book have been selected with an eye to the children's interests and their own specific level of development. In many instances the work is set in such a way that children cannot help but write the correct answers, for children learn by doing—but they learn more surely by doing correctly. The activities are presented in a simple and clear format thus ensuring only minimum guidance from the parent or teacher is required. In fact, organisation of this book encourages self-reliance through carefully graded exercises appropriate to the children's interests and levels of attainment.

It is important that parents and teachers monitor the child's progress, to make sure they are not working in areas above their ability. For example, if a Year 1 child is having difficulty with the grammar and punctuation sections, it would be best to leave these for a time and come back to them at a later stage in the year.

Peter Clutterbuck

ADDING INITIAL LETTERS

Choose the correct letter to complete each word.

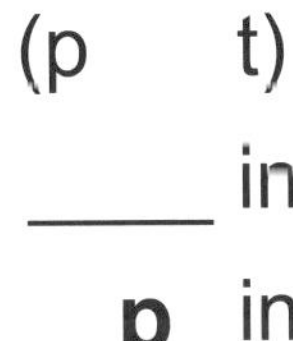

(p t)

____ in

__**p**__ in

1. (t m)

____ ap

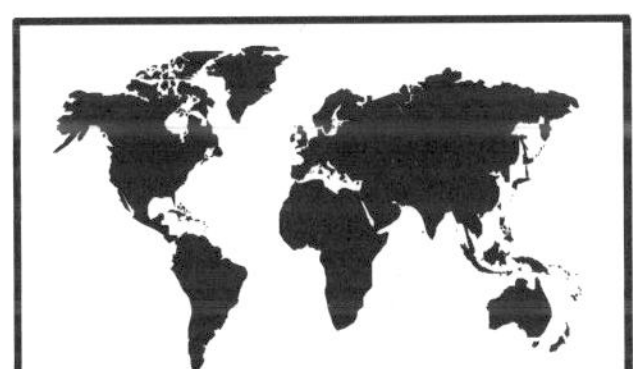

2. (f b)

____ ox

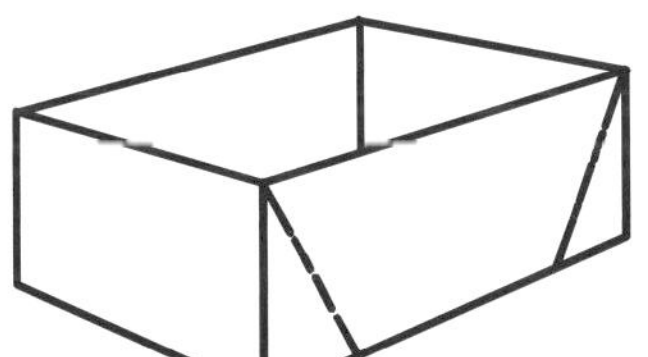

3. (g p)

____ ig

4. (h p)

____ en

5. (r c)

____at

6. (b f)

____ in

7. (r l)

____ og

8. (c h)

____ ot

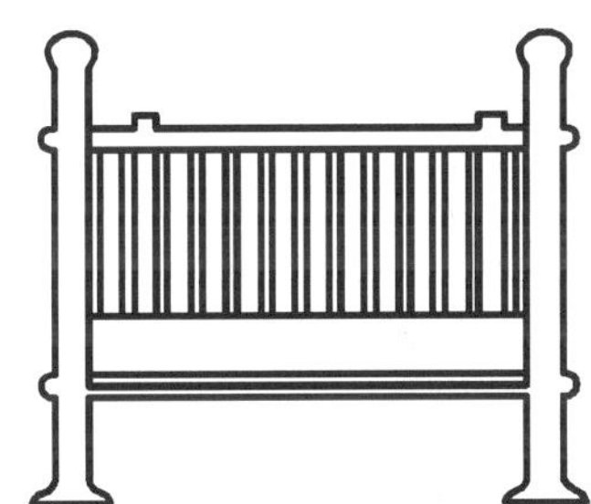

9. (b s)

____ it

10. (m t)

____ op

CHANGING FINAL LETTERS

If we change the last letter of a word we can make a new word.

ru**n**  ru**g** 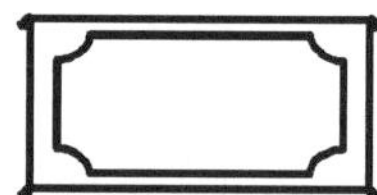

Change the last letter of each word to make a new word that fits the picture.

1. fat fa ______

2. bat ba ______

3. and an ______

4. ham ha ______

5. rag ra ______

 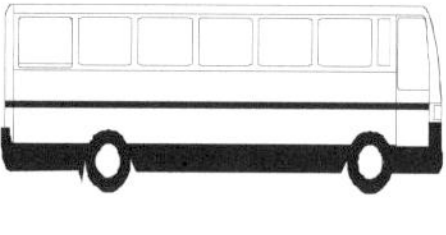

6. bug bu ______

7. peg pe ______

8. man ma______

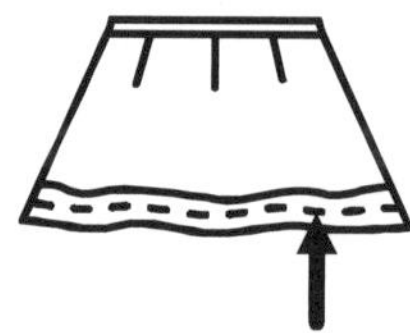 

9. hem he ______

10. fog fo ______

ADDING VOWELS

The vowels are a, e, i, o and u.

Add one of these in each space to complete the word.

Example d ____ g = d**o**g

1. b______ x

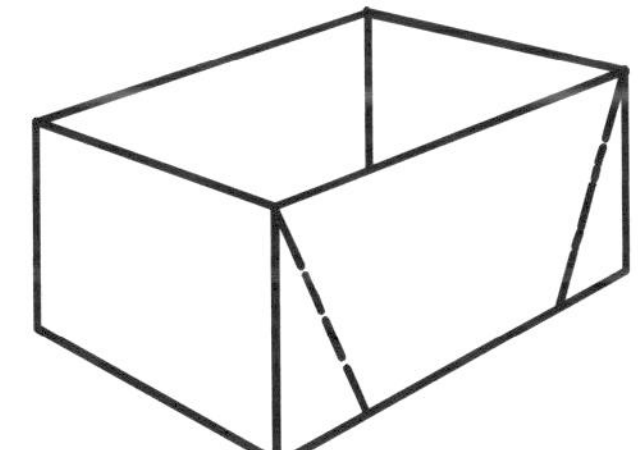

6. c______ p

2. n______ t

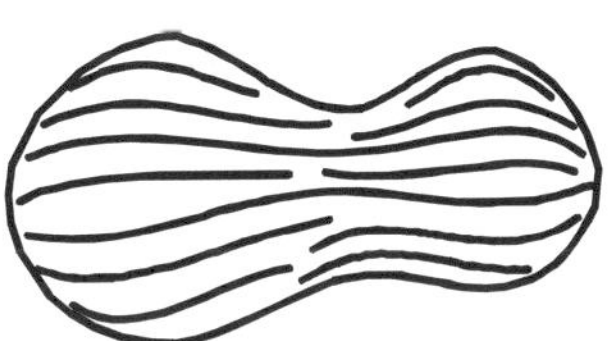

7. p ______ n

3. s______ x

8. p______ n

4. l ______ g

9. m ______ p

5. b______ g

10. r ______ g

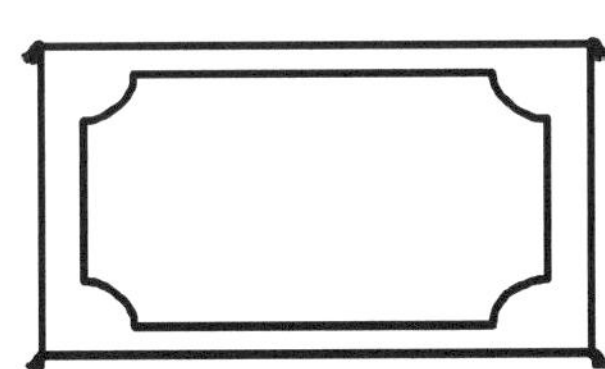

INITIAL BLENDS

Choose the correct letter group to complete each word.

1. (cl st)

_________ ock

2. (dr cr)

_________ um

3. (fl tr)

_________ ee

4. (tr fr)

_________ ain

5. (sk st)

_________ ar

6. (fl cr)

_________ y

7. (sp bl)

_________ oon

8. (bl gr)

_________ ub

9. (pl pr)

_________ ane

10. (st sp)

_________ op

FINAL BLENDS

Add the correct letters in the space. Draw a picture of the word you made.

1. (nt st)

   The camper was in the

   te________ .

2. (ft nd)

   I fell and hurt my ha________ .

3. (lt nk)

   I am wearing a be ________ around my waist.

4. (nt mp)

   An a________ has six legs.

5. (sk nt)

   Chicko is wearing a

   ma________ .

6. (mp nd)

   I put a sta________ on the

   envelope.

7. (nk st)

   I would like a dri________ of water.

8. (nk nd)

   The wi________ is blowing.

9. (ft st)

   Will you help me li________ the table?

10. (st nt)

    I made a fi________ with my

    hand.

DOUBLE LETTERS (CONSONANTS)

Add the correct set of double letters.

1. (ll mm)

Tai has a ba_______.

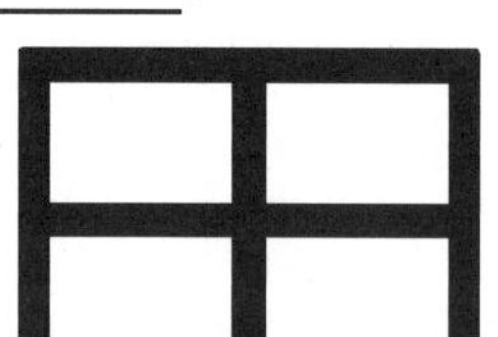

2. (ss tt)

A window is made of gla______.

3. (ll tt)

Gina rang the be_______.

4. (rr ll)

Tessa climbed a hi_______.

5. (ll pp)

Akako is playing with a do_____.

6. (pp mm)

A po_______y is a flower.

7. (tt pp)

There is water in the bo____le.

8. (ll mm)

A bu_______ is eating grass.

9. (gg tt)

Li is eating an e_______.

10. (ss tt)

A snake can hi_______.

DOUBLE LETTERS (VOWELS)

Add the correct set of double letters.

1. (ee oo)

A b_______ makes honey for us to eat.

2. (ee oo)

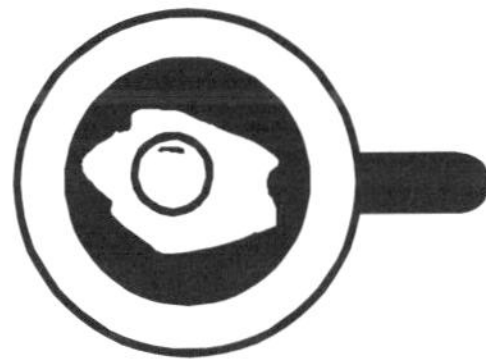

Melita is c_______ing an egg.

3. (ee oo)

This number is thr_______.

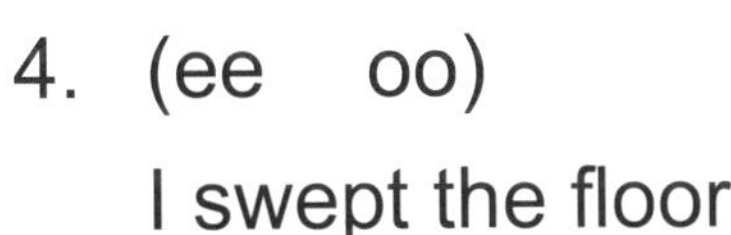
4. (ee oo)
I swept the floor

with a br_______m.

5. (ee oo)

A sh_______p gives us wool.

6. (ee oo)

Grass is gr_______n.

7. (ee oo)

Here is a tall tr_______.

8. (ee oo)

I can read a b_______k.

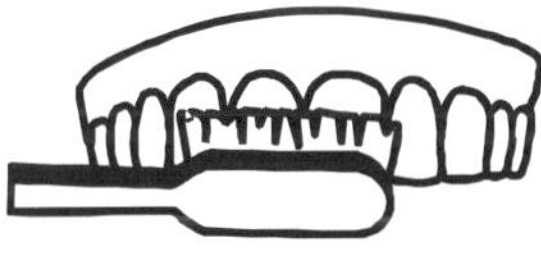

9. (ee oo)

I always clean my t_______
th.

10. (ee oo)

I eat with a sp_______n.

SIGHT WORDS

Write each word beside the correct picture.

1. pin a) ______________________

   peg b) ______________________

   pan c) ______________________

   pup d) ______________________

2. car a) ______________________

   arm b) ______________________

   star c) ______________________

   farm d) ______________________

3. cry a) ______________________

   dry b) ______________________

   fly c) ______________________

   sky d) ______________________

WORD BUILDING (1)

Use one letter from each box to make a word that matches the picture.

1.

c	u	g
l	a	s
b	e	r

a) ____________________

b) ____________________

c) ____________________

2.

b	g	g
e	e	g
p	i	d

a) ____________________

b) ____________________

c) ____________________

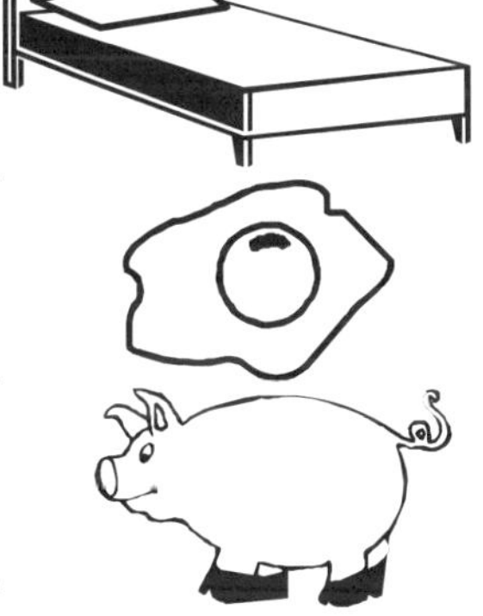

3.

r	e	t
h	a	p
c	u	n

a) ____________________

b) ____________________

c) ____________________

WORD BUILDING (2)

Join the pieces to make the words. Write the words. Draw a picture for each word. The first one is done for you.

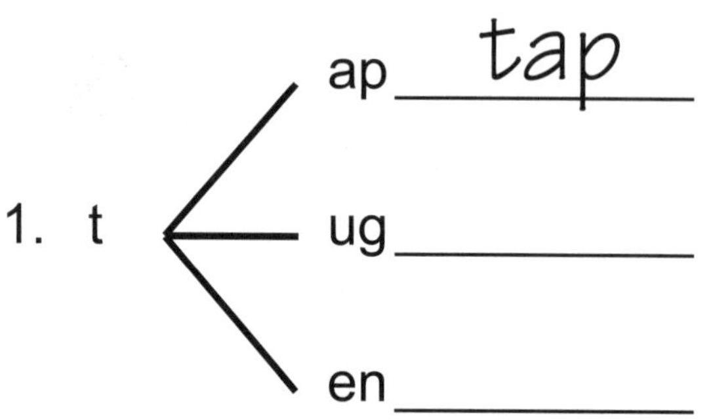

1. t
   - ap tap
   - ug ______
   - en ______

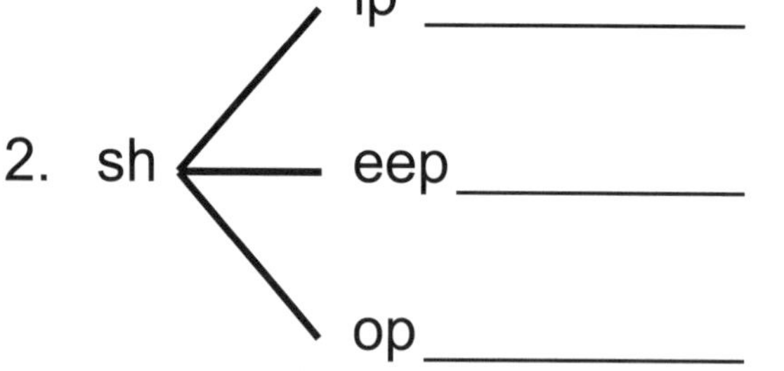

2. sh
   - ip ______
   - eep ______
   - op ______

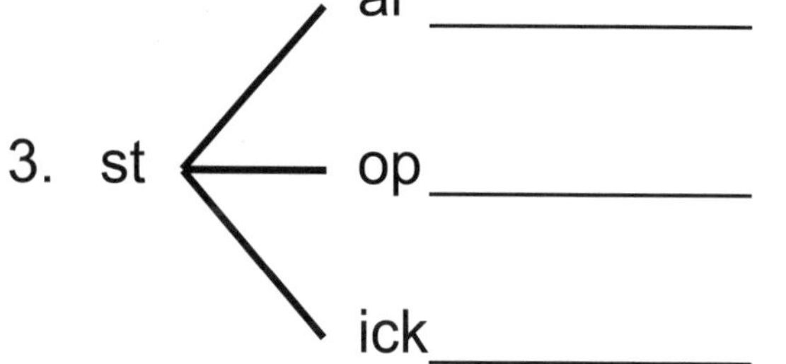

3. st
   - ar ______
   - op ______
   - ick ______

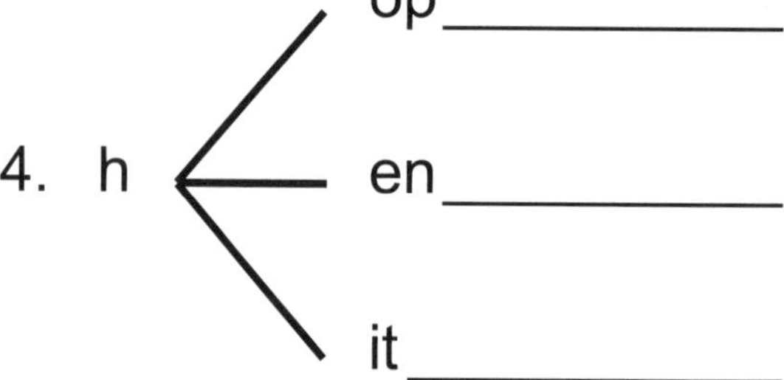

4. h
   - op ______
   - en ______
   - it ______

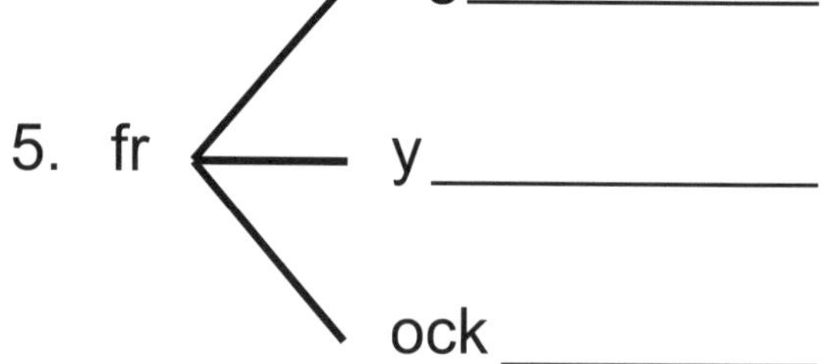

5. fr
   - og ______
   - y ______
   - ock ______

6. cr
   - ab ______
   - oss ______
   - y ______

WORD SHAPES

Choose the word that fits in each shape. Write it in the shape.

1.

leg

pin

2.

egg

ate

3.

old

pet

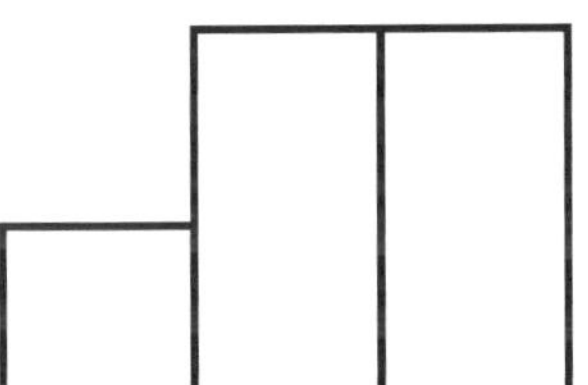

4.

toy

cow

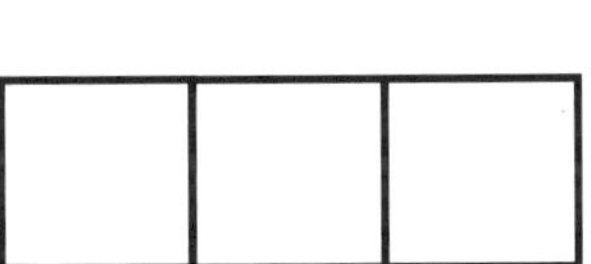

5.

sad

bad

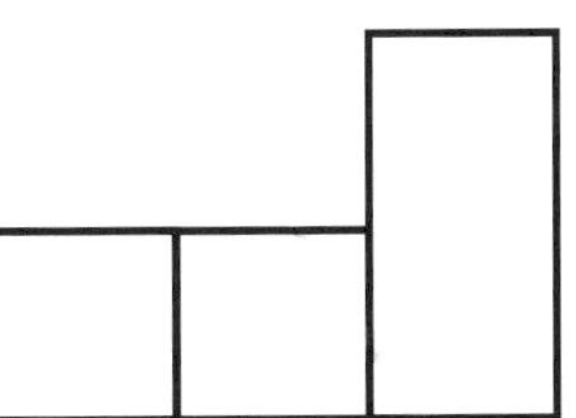

6.

hat

hay

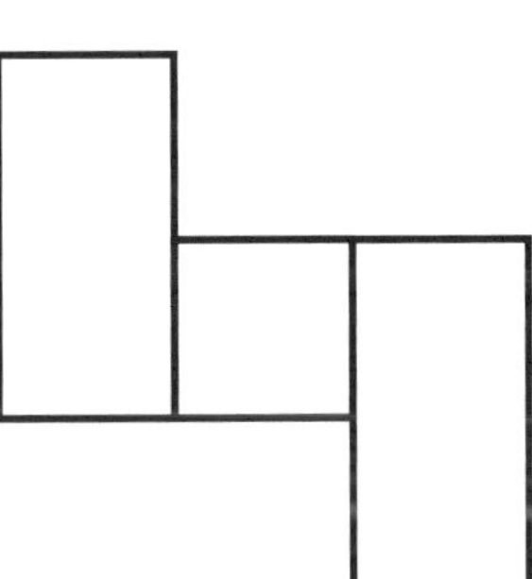

7.

ball

best

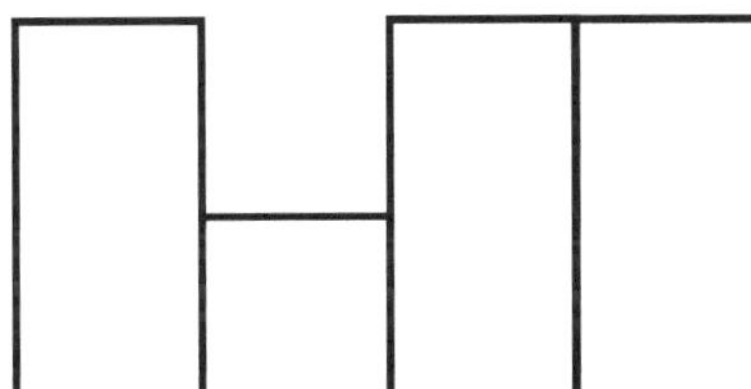

8.

milk

more

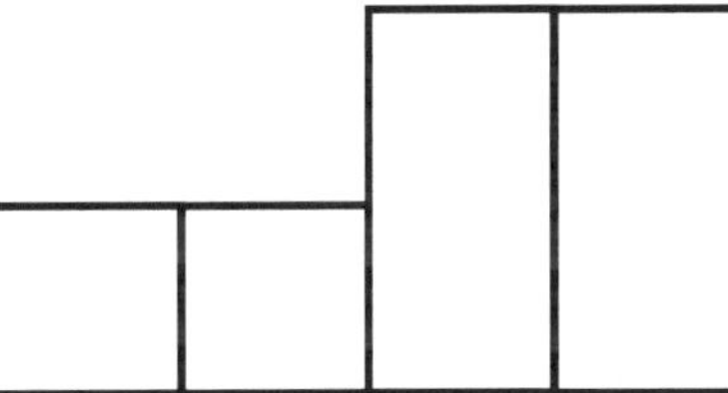

9.

send

shop

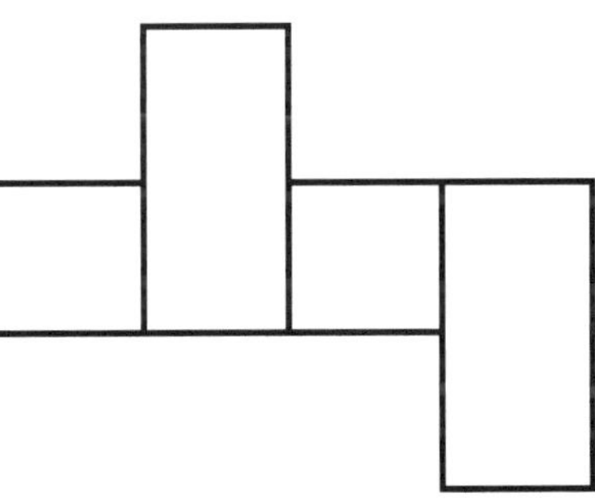

10.

nine

ring

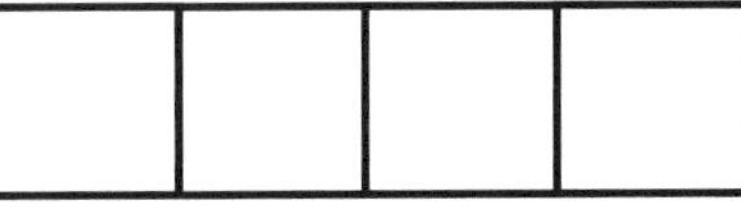

WORDS THAT SOUND THE SAME

Circle the two words that sound the same. Write a sentence with the two words.

1. hay day log

____

____

6. fox fan box

____

____

2. pig leg peg

____

____

7. wall sell call

____

____

3. sun bun ten

____

____

8. bell fell ball

____

____

4. toy gap boy

____

____

9. gold good told

____

____

9. bit sat hat

____

____

10. nest lost pest

____

____

SOUNDS

Add the correct sound in the space. Draw a picture of the word you make.

1. (ai ur)

   I can hammer in a n_______l.

2. (oy aw)

   This is my t_______.

3. (oa ue)

   The b_______t is on the water.

4. (ar ou)

   A m_______se ate the cheese.

5. (ir ou)

   A b_______d can fly.

6. (ow ar)

   I saw a cow at the f_______m.

7. (ar ou)

   We live in a big h_______se.

8. (ee oo)

   The m_______n is shining.

9. (or ie)

   I used a f_______k to eat my food.

10. (ew ay)

    I like to pl_______ games. Do you?

LETTER PATTERNS

Draw a line from the word to the picture.

1. fell

   bell

   sell

6. root

   boot

   soot

2. meat

   seat

   heat

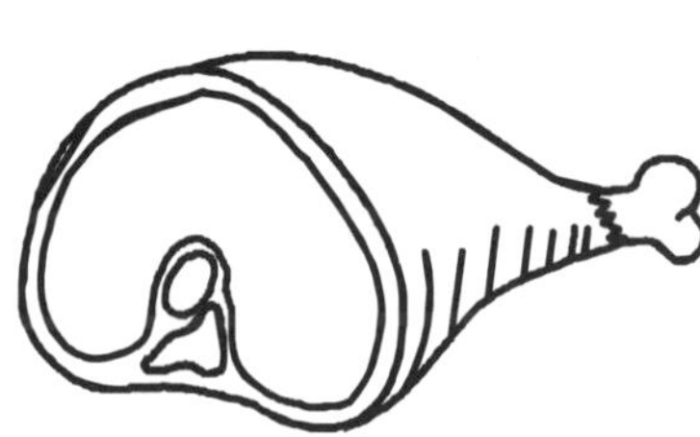

7. nice

   mice

   rice

3. sail

   mail

   tail

8. best

   test

   nest

4. cake

   make

   wake

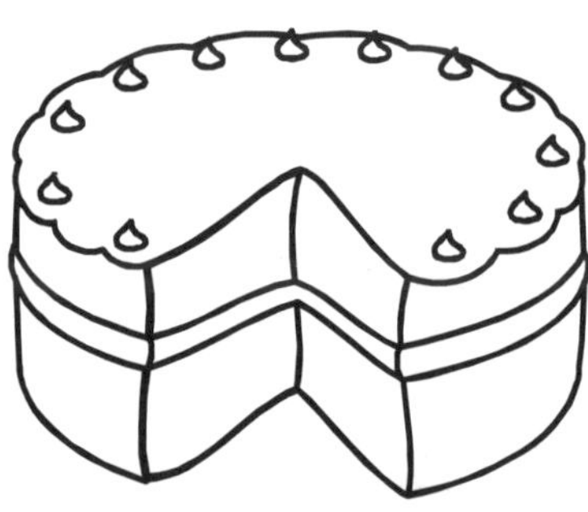

9. gate

   late

   mate

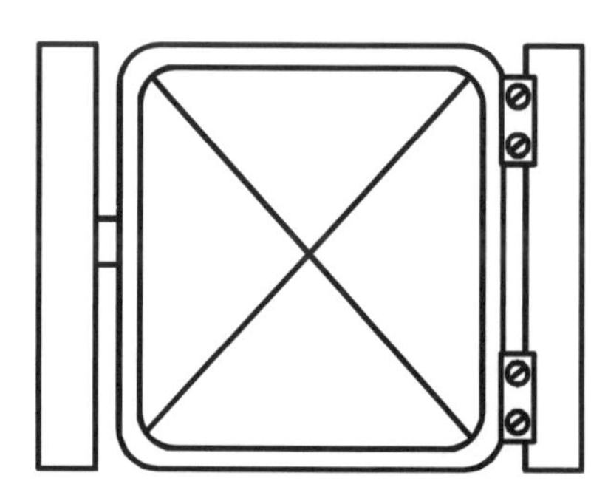

5. age

   page

   cage

10. tack

    sack

    back

JOINING WORD PIECES

Join the word pieces and write them in their correct order to make the word that matches the picture.

Example ip ch

chip

1. ag fl

____

2. um dr

____

3. ab cr

____

4. ip sh

____

5. ne ni

____

6. ng ri

____

7. nt te

____

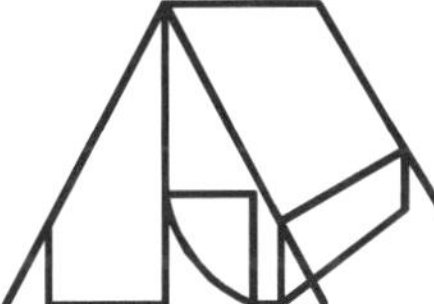

8. ck du

____

9. ng wi

____

10. lk mi

____

JUMBLED WORDS

Rearrange the letters to make the word that fits the picture. Write the word.

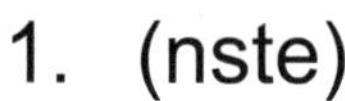

1. (nste) ____________

6. (lldo) ____________

2. (shfi) ____________

7. (arst) ____________

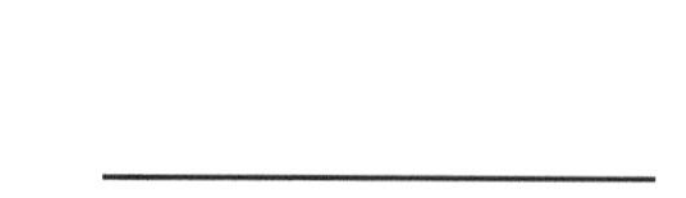

3. (ndwi) ____________

8. (edsh) ____________

4. (llwa) ____________

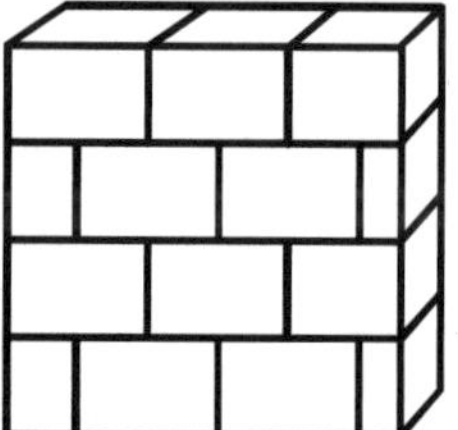

9. (thmo) ____________

5. (ocw) ____________

10. (cklo) ____________

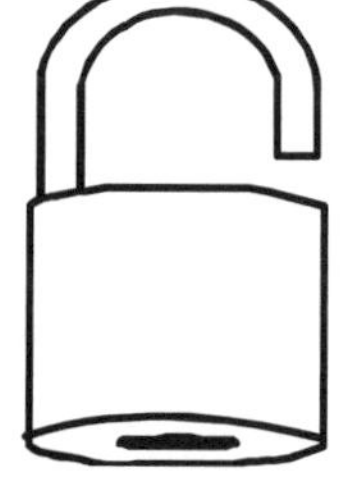

PLURAL WORDS

To make a noun mean **more than one** we add **s** to the end of the word.

Example one cat two cat**s**

Add an s to each word to make each word mean more than one.

1. one hat two __________
6. one bag three __________

   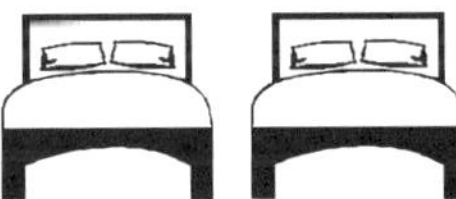

2. one hill four __________
7. one bed two __________

   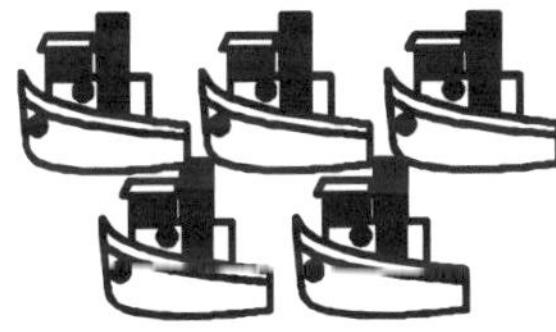

3. one doll three __________
8. one ship five __________

   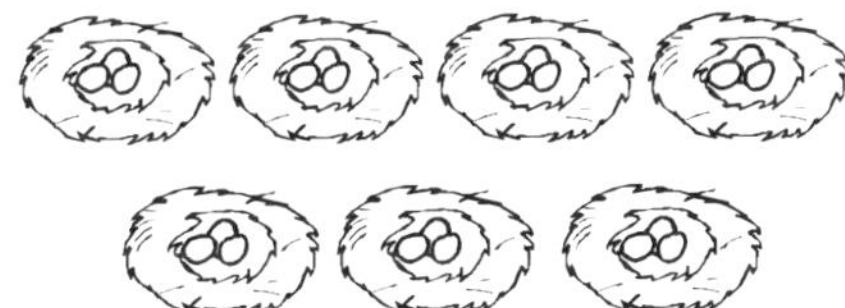

4. one coat two __________
9. one nest seven __________

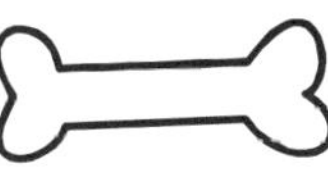  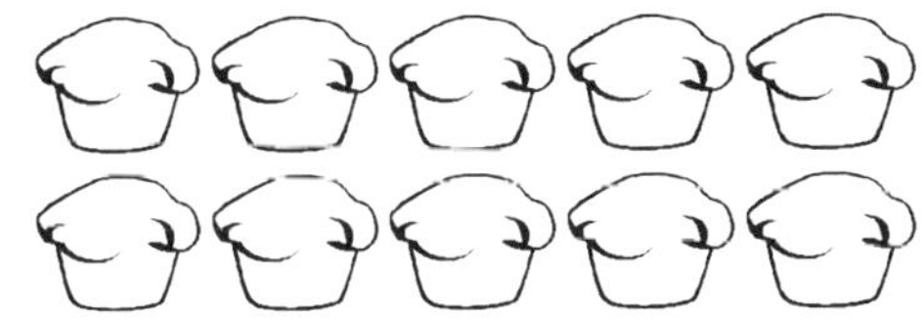

5. one bone three __________
10. one cake ten __________

WORDS FOR PICTURES

Fill in the missing words using the picture clues.

dog	hen	pig	sun

One day a ______________ and a ______________ went for a walk in the hot ______________ . They saw a ______________ eating a bone.

tree	bird	egg	nest

A ______________ made its ______________ in a ______________ . It laid an ______________ in the nest.

bed	stars	cow	car

My mother took me in the ______________ to see a ______________ that was on a farm. When we got home it was dark. The ______________ were twinkling so I went to ______________ .

COMPOUND WORDS

Add a word from the box to complete each compound word.

lace	cup	fish	brush
corn	fly	ball	set

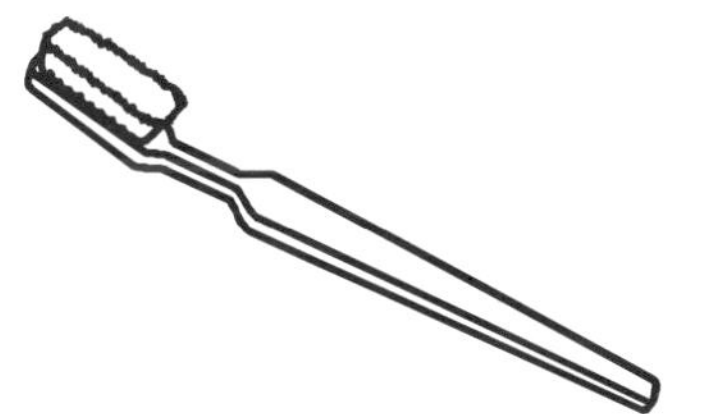

1. tooth ________________

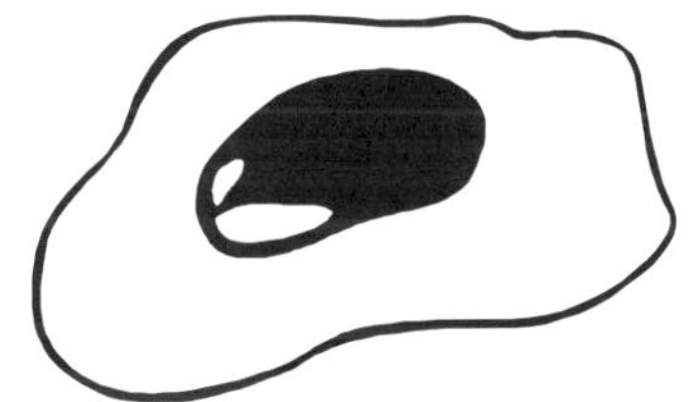

2. egg ________________

3. pop ________________

4. sun ________________

5. shoe ________________

6. star ________________

7. butter ________________

8. foot ________________

OPPOSITES

Words can be **opposite**. An opposite word means what the first word doesn't mean.

Example up ↑ down ↓

Draw a line to match each word to its opposite.

hot	wet
dry	slow
big	cold
fast	little

Choose a word from the box to fill the spaces.

fat	shut	hard	black

This door is open  but this one is ________________ . 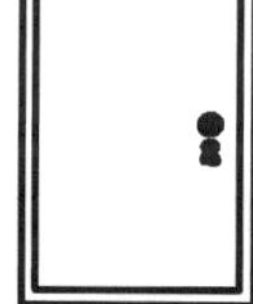

This dog is thin  but this pig is ________________ . 

This is white 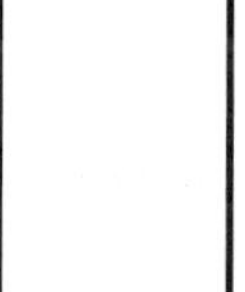 and this is ________________ . 

Wool is soft  but a rock is ________________ . 

HOMOPHONES

Homophones are words that **sound** the same but have different spellings and different meanings.

Colour the box that has the correct word.

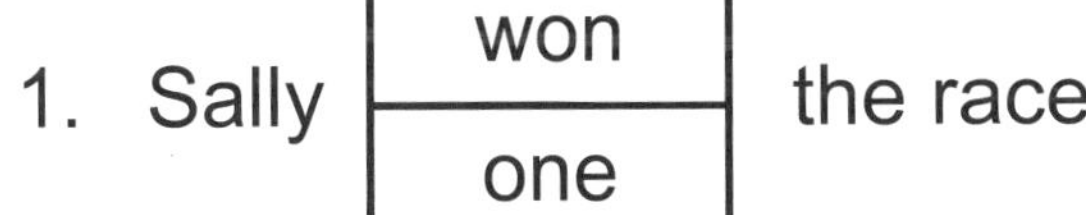

1. Sally [won / one] the race.

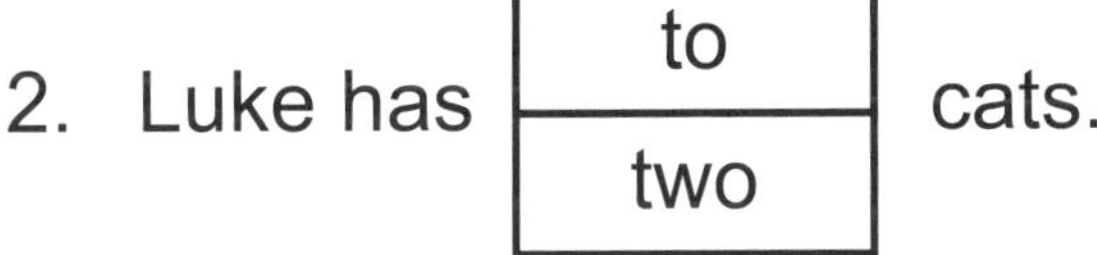

2. Luke has [to / two] cats.

3. The [sun / son] is hot.

4. I saw [for / four] birds.

5. Kayla swam in the [sea / see] .

6. A dog has a [tale / tail] .

7. We only have [one / won] dog.

8. A [bee / be] makes honey for us.

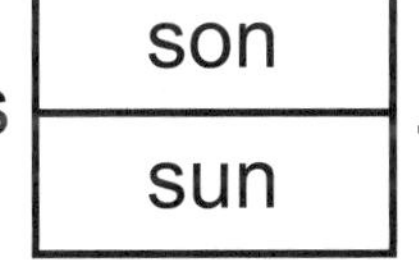

9. John is Mr Smith's [son / sun] .

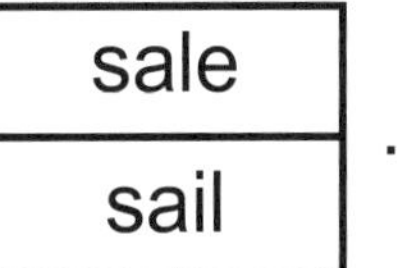

10. A ship has a [sale / sail] .

ANAGRAMS

Anagrams are words made from the same letters as another word.

Rearrange the letters of each word to make a word that fits the picture.

1. This is a **pat**. ____________

2. This is a **tar**. ____________

3. This is a **tab**. ____________

4. This is a **sub**. ____________

5. This is an **ram**. ____________

6. This is a **god**. ____________

7. This is a **nip**. ____________

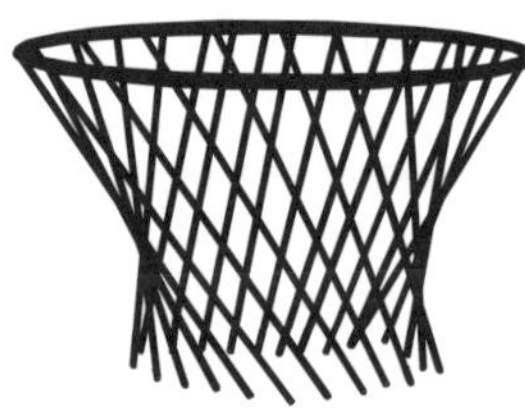

8. This is a **ten**. ____________

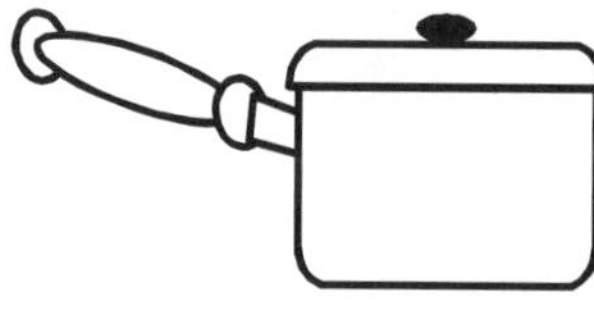

9. This is a **top**. ____________

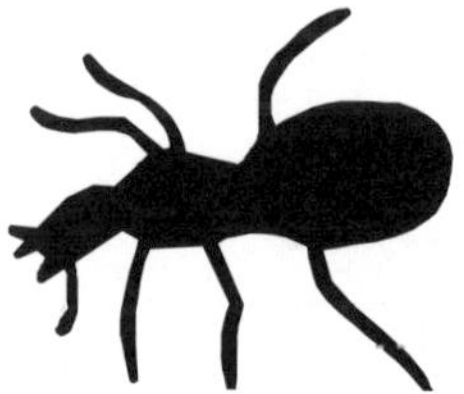

10. This is an **tan**. ____________

WORDS WITH THE SAME MEANING

Some words have the same or nearly the same meaning.

Example **little** and **small** mean the same thing.

Draw a line to match each word to one that means the same.

happy	stone
big	trip
rock	glad
fall	large

Match a word from the box to each sentence that has the same or nearly the same meaning as the word underlined.

sick	fix	rest	fast

1. I am going to <u>mend</u> the door. ____________________
2. Chan is going to have a <u>sleep</u>. ____________________
3. Jake is feeling <u>unwell</u>. He feels ____________________.
4. Akako is a <u>quick</u> runner. ____________________

DROPPING LETTERS

Sometimes we can drop a letter from a word to leave a word that has a different meaning.

Example ~~g~~old old

Drop a letter from each word to leave one that matches the picture.

1. card ________________

2. bring________________

3. stop ________________

4. cape________________

5. spin ________________

6. spot ________________

7. pink ________________

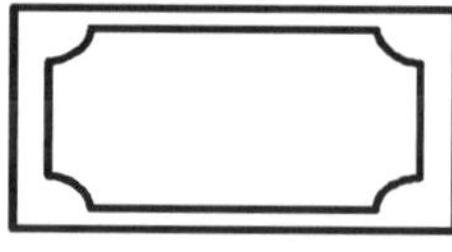

8. mate________________

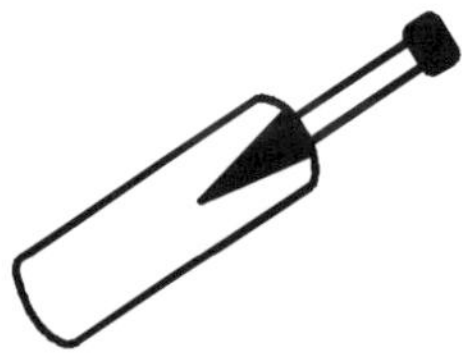

9. bath ________________

10. farm ________________

WORD MEANINGS

Sort the words in the box into groups and write them under the headings.

boots	cakes	jam	butter
jumper	buns	socks	jeans

Things We Eat

Things We Wear

Sort the words in the box into groups and write them under the headings.

cow	blue	green	horse
dog	red	zebra	yellow

Colours

Animals

INITIAL BLENDS

Choose the two letters that begin each word. Write them in the space.

1. (fl bl)

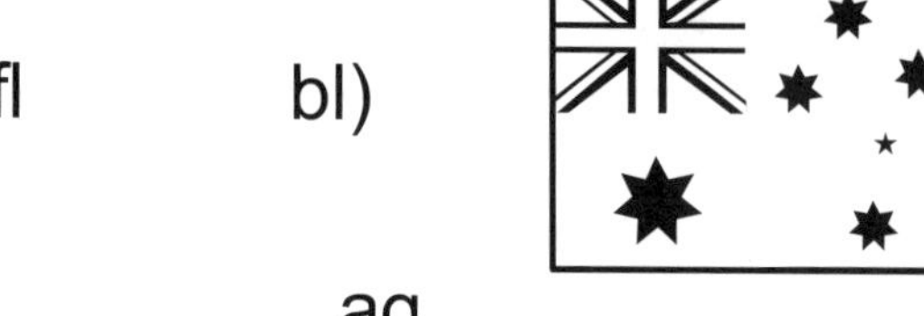

__________ag

2. (cr dr)

__________ess

3. (st br)

__________ick

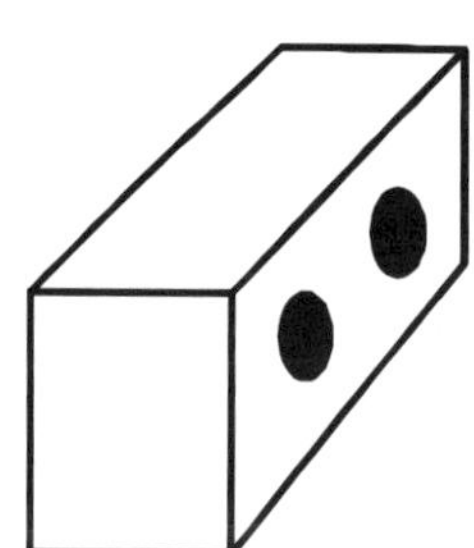

4. (pr sl)

__________am

5. (cr cl)

__________eek

6. (cr gr)

__________ab

7. (cr cl)

__________own

8. (br bl)

__________ush

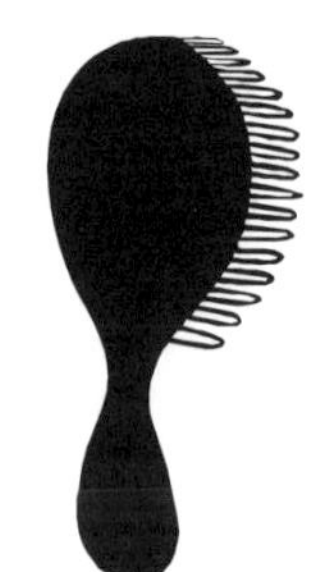

9. (sr tr)

__________ain

10. (pl pr)

__________ant

FINAL BLENDS

Choose the correct pair of letters to complete each word.

1. The ducks are on the po________.
(st nd)

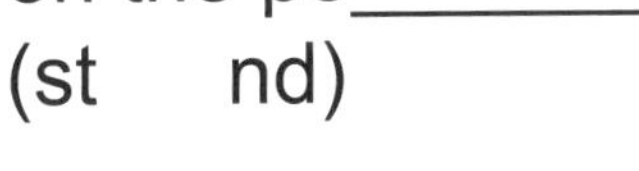

2. An elephant has a tu________.
(sk nd)

3. I need a sta________.
(mp sk)

4. Please turn on the la________.
(mp st)

5. That is a big bo________.
(mt lt)

6. For her birthday I gave Sally a gi________.
(st ft)

7. Wool is so________.
(ft nd)

8. Can you ju________ over the fence?
(lt mp)

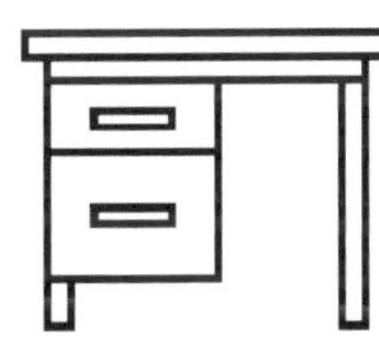

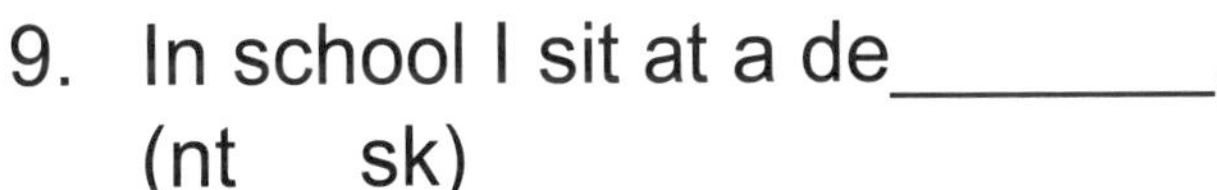

9. In school I sit at a de________.
(nt sk)

10. A young horse is called a co________.
(lt sk)

SOUNDS

Say each word out loud.

ai

rain	nail	train	tail	sail	snail

Choose a word from the box to finish each sentence.

1. The hammer pushed the __________ into the wood.
2. I found a__________ on the leaf.
3. We caught the __________ at the station.
4. A fox has a bushy ________ .
5. This boat has a small __________.
6. In the morning it began to __________ .

Say each word out loud.

ow

yellow	grow	throw	slow	snow	show

Choose a word from the box to finish each sentence.

1. Do not __________that stone at the window.
2. On a very cold day it will sometimes __________ .
3. A rabbit is quick but a snail is __________ .
4. If you plant a seed it might __________.
5. A ripe banana has a __________ skin.
6. I wanted to __________ my friends my new bike.

WORD BUILDING

Add the correct letter pair to complete the word. Write it in the space.

1. (or ir)

b_________d

2. (ck sh)

du_________

3. (cr cl)

_________ock

4. (tw tr)

_________enty

5. (ea ee)

br_________k

6. (tr cl)

_________actor

7. (oo ee)

sp_________n

8. (ai oi)

ch_________n

9. (ai oi)

b_________l

10. (ou or)

h_________se

PROBLEM WORDS

Some words cause us problems when we spell them.

Circle the correct spelling of each word. Write the word in the space.

1. Do you (want wont) some more cake?

 ____

2. Tori knows I (like lick) eating ice-cream.

 ____

3. Who came (first frist) in the race?

 ____

4. Are you going to (cum come) to my party?

 ____

5. P.J. is sitting (wif with) Kanya.

 ____

6. Are (thay they) in the room?

 ____

7. The number after one is (to two).

 ____

8. Bruno (sed said) he would come with us.

 ____

9. You must clean your teeth (befor before) going to bed.

 ____

10. Jenny is (jist just) coming now.

 ____

11. We saw (sum some) big birds.

 ____

12. Come and (look luk) over here!

 ____

LETTER PATTERNS

Add the correct letter pattern to complete each word.

1. In the garden there is a

   sn______.

   (ale ail)

2. A cow has h______.

   (orns oots)

3. This is a big tr______.

   (uck ick)

4. Mike is wearing a c______.

   (ool oat)

5. I helped my father cut the

   w______.

   (one ood)

6. Amanda is wearing a

   m______.

   (ast ask)

7. Tom is eating a loaf of br______.

   (aid ead)

8. A sh______ gives us wool.

   (eer eep)

9. A bird builds a n______.

   (ast est)

10. I put the food on the

    pl______.

    (ave ate)

IDENTIFYING WORDS

Write the correct word.

1. The bird is in the________.

   (cage cake)

2. Uma can push the ________.

   (pram tram)

3. Tim shut the ________.

   (hate gate)

4. Last night I saw a ________.

   (star scar)

5. A cat caught a ________.

   (mouse house)

6. At the circus there was a

   ________. (down clown)

7. A ________ can fly.

   (path moth)

8. I swept the floor with a

   ________. (broom spoon)

9. She dug the hole with a

   ________. (spade made)

10. We sat in the ________ of the

    tree. (blade shade)

11. I got a letter in the ________.

    (pail mail)

12. The flour is made from

    ________. (cheat wheat)

ANSWERS

YEAR 1 SPELLING & VOCABULARY

Unit 1 Adding Initial Letters
1. map 2. box 3. pig 4. pen
5. rat 6. bin 7. log 8. cot
9. sit 10. mop

Unit 2 Changing Last Letters
1. fan 2. bag 3. ant 4. hat
5. rat 6. bus 7. pet 8. mat
9. hen 10. fox

Unit 3 Adding Vowels
1. box 2. nut 3. six 4. leg
5. bag 6. cap 7. pen 8. pin
9. mop 10. rug

Unit 4 Initial Blends
1. clock 2. drum 3. tree 4. train
5. star 6. fly 7. spoon 8. grub
9. plane 10. stop

Unit 5 Final Blends
1. tent 2. hand 3. belt 4. ant
5. mask 6. stamp 7. drink 8. wind
9. lift 10. fist

Unit 6 Double Letters (Consonants)
1. ball 2. glass 3. bell 4. hill
5. doll 6. poppy 7. bottle 8. bull
9. egg 10. hiss

Unit 7 Double Letters (Vowels)
1. bee 2. cooking 3. three 4. broom
5. sheep 6. green 7. tree 8. book
9. teeth 10. spoon

Unit 8 Sight Words
1.a) pan b) pup c) pin d) peg
2.a) arm b) car c) farm d) star
3.a) dry b) fly c) sky d) cry

Unit 9 Word Building (1)
1.a) car b) leg c) bus
2.a) bed b) egg c) pig
3.a) rat b) hen c) cup

Unit 10 Word Building (2)
1. tap tug ten 2. ship sheep shop
3. star stop stick 4. hop hen hit
5. frog fry frock 6. crab cross cry

Unit 11 Word Shapes
1. pin 2. egg 3. old 4. cow
5. sad 6. hay 7. ball 8. milk
9. shop 10. nine

Unit 12 Words that Sound the Same
1. hay day 2. leg peg 3. sun bun
4. toy boy 5. sat hat 6. fox box
7. wall call 8. bell fell 9. gold told
10. nest pest

Unit 13 Sounds
1. nail 2. toy 3. boat 4. mouse
5. bird 6. farm 7. house 8. moon
9. fork 10. play

Unit 14 Letter Patterns
1. bell 2. meat 3. tail 4. cake
5. cage 6. boot 7. mice 8. nest
9. gate 10. tack

Unit 15 Joining Word Pieces
1. flag 2. drum 3. crab 4. ship
5. nine 6. ring 7. tent 8. duck
9. wing 10. milk

Unit 16 Jumbled Words
1. nest 2. fish 3. wind 4. wall
5. cow 6. doll 7. star 8. shed
9. moth 10. lock

Unit 17 Plural Words
1. hats 2. hills 3. dolls 4. coats
5. bones 6. bags 7. beds 8. ships
9. nests 10. cakes

YEAR 1 VOCABULARY

Unit 18 Words For Pictures
hen pig sun dog
bird nest tree egg
car cow stars bed

Unit 19 Compound Words
1. toothbrush 2. eggcup 3. popcorn
4. sunset 5. shoelace 6. starfish
7. butterfly 8. football

Unit 20 Opposites
(hot cold) (dry wet) (big little) (fast slow)
shut fat black hard

Unit 21 Homophones
1. won 2. two 3. sun 4. four
5. sea 6. tail 7. one 8. bee
9. son 10. sail

Unit 22 Anagrams
1. tap 2. rat 3. bat 4. bus
5. arm 6. dog 7. pin 8. net
9. pot 10. ant

Unit 23 Words with the Same Meaning
A. (happy glad) (big large)
(rock stone) (fall trip)
B. 1. fix 2. rest
3. sick 4. fast

Unit 24 Dropping Letters
1. car 2. ring 3. top 4. cap
5. pin 6. pot 7. ink 8. mat
9. bat 10. arm

Unit 25 Word Meanings

Things We Eat	*Things We Wear*
cakes	boots
jam	jumper
butter	socks
buns	jeans

Colours		*Animals*	
blue	red	cow	horse
green	yellow	dog	zebra

YEAR 2 SPELLING

Unit 26 Initial Blends
1. flag 2. dress 3. brick 4. pram
5. creek 6. crab 7. clown 8. brush
9. train 10. plant

Unit 27 Final Blends
1. pond 2. tusk 3. stamp 4. lamp
5. bolt 6. gift 7. soft 8. jump
9. desk 10. colt

Unit 28 Sounds
ai sounds:
1. nail 2. snail 3. train
4. tail 5. sail 6. rain
ow sounds:
1. throw 2. snow 3. slow
4. grow 5. yellow 6. show

Unit 29 Word Building
1. bird 2. duck 3. clock 4. twenty
5. break 6. tractor 7. spoon 8. chain
9. boil 10. horse

Unit 30 Problem Words
1. want 2. like 3. first 4. come
5. with 6. they 7. two 8. said
9. before 10. just 11. some 12. look

Unit 31 Letter Patterns
1. snail 2. horns 3. truck 4. coat
5. wood 6. mask 7. bread 8. sheep
9. nest 10. plate

Unit 32 Identifying Words
1. cage 2. pram 3. gate 4. star
5. mouse 6. clown 7. moth 8. broom
9. spade 10. shade 11. mail 12. wheat

Unit 33 Double Letters
1. bell 2. hammer 3. summer 4. dinner
5. kitten 6. lolly 7. little 8. ball
9. happy 10. pillow

Unit 34 Base Words
1. shop 2. trick 3. pull 4. cover
5. step 6. weep 7. trot 8. paint
9. clap 10. scrub 11. watch 12. toast

Unit 35 Small Words
1. toes 2. name 3. last 4. ten
5. light 6. bin 7. well 8. tractor
9. tell 10. cup 11. air 12. race

Unit 36 Adding Letters
1. sheep 2. frog 3. ship 4. clock
5. shell 6. boat 7. four 8. tree
9. nest 10. coat 11. snow 12. mouth

Unit 37 Letter Pieces
1. book nine 2. bear moon 3. ring drum
4. ship nest 5. bone star 6. baby bird
7. duck shed 8. card cake 9. gate seed
10. door bush 11. shoe hair 12. race meat

Unit 38 Syllables
1. kangaroo 2. holiday 3. December
4. elephant 5. skeleton 6. calendar
7. lemonade 8. yesterday 9. animal
10. dinosaur

Unit 39 Silent Letters
1. climb 2. lamb 3. whole 4. knee
5. ghost 6. castle 7. calf 8. write
9. wrap 10. knife

Unit 40 Plural Words
1. birds 2. apples 3. books 4. cows
5. keys 6. trays 7. toys 8. donkeys
9. glasses 10. watches 11. bushes 12. buses

Unit 41 Spelling Rules (1)
1. dropped 2. stopped 3. dragged 4. rubbed
5. plugged 6. hopped 7. mopped 8. chopped
9. skipped 10. tapped

Unit 42 Spelling Rules (2)
1. shopping 2. stepping 3. swimming
4. humming 5. cutting 6. running
7. digging 8. sitting 9. patting
10. getting

YEAR 2 VOCABULARY

Unit 43 Compound Words
1. pigtails 2. birthday 3. goldfish
4. pancakes 5. seaweed 6. butterfly
7. flowerpot 8. football 9. grasshopper
10. tablecloth

Unit 44 Opposites
1. dirty 2. buy 3. short 4. cold
5. shut 6. lost 7. laugh 8. take
9. old 10. stop

Unit 45 Homophones
1. four 2. tail 3. to 4. hear
5. sun 6. meet 7. week 8. wood
9. sell 10. buy

ANSWERS

Unit 46 **Anagrams**

1. cat 2. arm 3. won 4. tap
5. owl 6. saw 7. tea 8. saw
9. pin 10. tub

Unit 47 **Words with the Same Meaning**

1. damp 2. begin 3. sick 4. sad
5. yell 6. nasty 7. small 8. close
9. quickly 10. dress

Unit 48 **Word Meanings - Places**

1. hospital 2. airport 3. bed 4. store
5. beach 6. garage 7. bridge 8. garden
9. school 10. zoo

Unit 49 **Word Families**

Birds	***Insects***	***Animals***
magpie	ant	camel
owl	grasshopper	donkey
emu	butterfly	zebra
Flowers	***Vegetables***	***Colours***
rose	carrot	yellow
daisy	beans	orange
daffodil	potato	purple

Unit 50 **Similes**

1. grass 2. bee 3. snow 4. owl
5. nails 6. rake 7. lion 8. feather
9. mouse 10. toast
11 - 14. Parent/Teacher correction

YEARS 1 & 2 GRAMMAR

Unit 51 **Using a or an before Words**

1. an 2. an 3. a 4. a
5. a 6. a 7. a 8. an
9. a 10. an

Unit 52 **Nouns (1)**

1. tub 2. wall 3. corner 4. hill
5. shoe 6. sty 7. stable 8. web
9. shell 10. nest

Unit 53 **Nouns (2)**

In the kitchen	***In the bathroom***	***In the garden***
kettle	shower	tree
stove	bath	flower
freezer	soap	spade

(bottle glass) (jumper wool)
(book paper) (table wood)
(ball rubber)

Unit 54 **Verbs**

sitting playing crying
skipping jumping riding

1. sweep 2. ride 3. fly
4. post 5. wash 6. dig

Unit 55 **Verbs - Tense**

1. digging 2. riding 3. eating
4. sweeping 5. playing 6. driving

1. ate 2. walk 3. went
4. win 5. fell 6. help

Unit 56 **Using is and are**

1. is 2. are 3. are 4. are
5. is 6. are 7. are 8. is

Using was and were

1. was 2. were 3. was 4. was
5. were 6. was 7. were 8. was

Unit 57 **Adjectives**

1. hot 2. cold 3. soft
4. big 5. small 6. red

1. blue 2. yellow 3. fast
4. shut 5. old 6. sharp

Unit 58 **Adverbs**

1. tonight 2. fast 3. inside
4. still 5. yesterday 6. here
7. soon 8. slowly 9. today
10. sadly

Unit 59 **Prepositions**

1. up 2. on 3. behind
4. beside 5. between 6. over
7. above

Unit 60 **Pronouns**

1. He, They 2. her, They 3. It, He
4. They, her 5. She, her 6. She, me
7. They, them 8. ours, you

Unit 61 **Conjunctions**

1. and 2. unless 3. if
4. until 5. because 6. since
7. for 8. who 9. but
10. that

Unit 62 **Phrases**

1. last Tuesday 2. in the kennel
3. in the park 4. in a bed
5. at nine o'clock 6. with the long tail
7. under the rock 8. with the long beard
9. at the station 10. at four o'clock

Unit 63 **Sentences**

1. a 2. a 3. b 4. a
5. b 6. a 7. a 8. a
9. a 10. a

ANSWERS

YEARS 1 & 2 PUNCTUATION

Unit 64 Statements

1. The dog is in the car.
2. That is a big tree.
3. It is nearly time to go.
4. He is in the room.
5. She is playing a game.
6. My cat is called Fluffy.
7. My father did the dishes.
8. I put the cup on the bench.
9. This is an old table.
10. Go to your room now.

Unit 65 Questions

1. What time is it?
2. Where is our teacher?
3. Where is the pencil you borrowed?
4. When will he get here?
5. Does Jared play tennis?
6. How did Elly get here so early?
7. Why did you do that?
8. What type of animal is a horse?
9. When will it be lunchtime?
10. Why are you climbing the tree?
11. Do you like eating pizza?
12. Is Tai your sister?

Unit 66 Statements and Questions

1. Where did David go?
   It is getting cold.
2. I haven't seen Matthew today.
   The old man rode a bicycle.
3. This tree has brown leaves.
   I put the book on the table.
4. Do you like apples?
   The dog is in the kennel.
5. Does your mother drive a car?
   Where is your new bike?

Unit 66 Statements and Questions Cont.

6. Where has Sally gone?
   My best friend is Paul.
7. They are jumping over the rope.
   He is sitting on the seat.
8. Who stole the diamonds?
   What day is it today?
9. A rose is a flower.
   A pig is an animal.
10. My favourite food is pizza.
    What time is it?

Unit 67 Statements, Questions & Exclamations

1. Our school has ten teachers.
2. What a lovely day!
3. Look out!
4. Where did you get the pie?
5. Why did you call Sam?
6. How terrible!
7. What time are we leaving?
8. I caught three fish yesterday.
9. This is an interesting book.
10. When did the bell ring?

Unit 68 Commas

1. My best friends are Terri, Elsa, Bruno and Sadiki.
2. The colours on the flag are red, blue, green and yellow.
3. I like to eat apples, pears, bananas and apricots.
4. Bees, ants, butterflies and wasps are all types of insects.
5. A carpenter uses a hammer, nails, a saw and a chisel.
6. Lin likes to play soccer, tennis, netball and cricket.
7. In my desk there are pens, pencils, books and erasers.
8. Magpies, ducks, geese and swans are all types of birds.

DOUBLE LETTERS

The words are missing their double letters. Write the sentence again with the right spelling.

1. (ll rr)

   Adam rang the be______.

   ____

2. (mm dd)

   I hit the nail with a ha______er.

   ____

3. (mm nn)

   It is hot in su______er.

   ____

4. (mm nn)

   I ate all my di______er.

   ____

5. (tt pp)

   Kayla has a ki______en.

   ____

6. (ss ll)

   I would like a lo______ y.

   ____

7. (tt nn)

   A mouse is li______le.

   ____

8. (ll dd)

   A ba______ will bounce.

   ____

9. (mm pp)

   Sean is very ha______y today.

   ____

10. (ll tt)

   I sleep on a pi______ow.

   ____

BASE WORDS

Lots of words we use are made from **base** words.
We can add **ed** or **ing** to base words to make bigger words.

Example lift**ed** comes from **lift**
smell**ing** comes from **smell**

Write the base word from which each word is made.

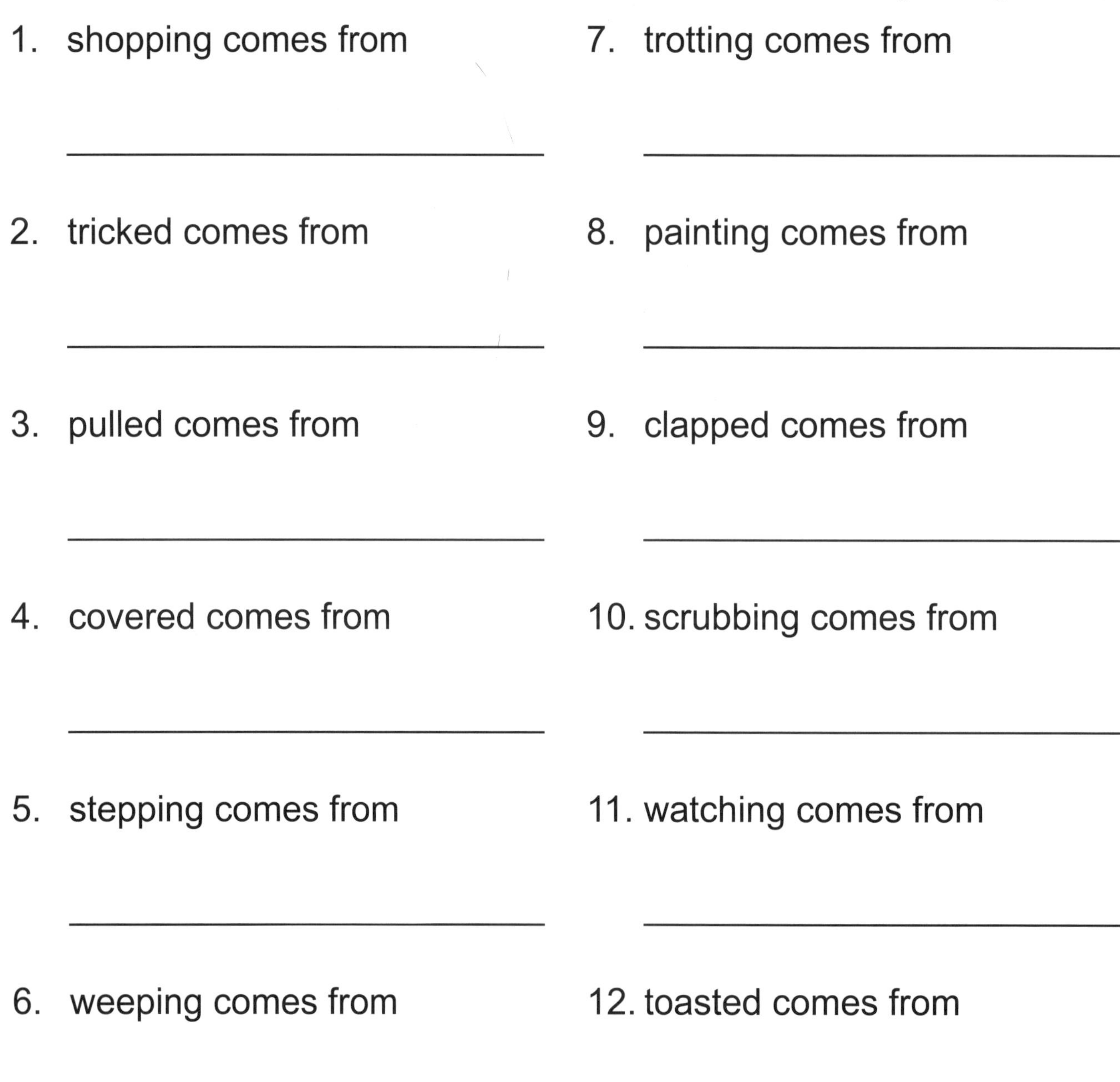

1. shopping comes from ______________________
2. tricked comes from ______________________
3. pulled comes from ______________________
4. covered comes from ______________________
5. stepping comes from ______________________
6. weeping comes from ______________________
7. trotting comes from ______________________
8. painting comes from ______________________
9. clapped comes from ______________________
10. scrubbing comes from ______________________
11. watching comes from ______________________
12. toasted comes from ______________________

SMALL WORDS

Each of the large words at the end of the sentence has a small word inside it. Write the small word in the space.

1. I have ten ________ on my feet. (tomatoes)
2. What is your ________? (enamel)
3. Who came ________ in the race? (elastic)
4. The number after nine is ________. (centenary)
5. Please switch on the ________. (delighted)
6. Put the papers in the ________. (cabinet)
7. Tania was ill but she is feeling ________ now. (jewellery)
8. A farmer ploughs with a ________. (protractor)
9. Will you ________ them I've arrived? (satellite)
10. I poured the hot tea into the ________. (occupation)
11. The ________ is crisp and clear today. (fairy)
12. Who won the ________? (bracelet)

ADDING LETTERS

Add a letter to each word to make a new word that matches the picture.

1. seep

____

2. fog

____

3. sip

____

4. lock

____

5. sell

____

6. bat

____

7. for

____

8. tee

____

9. net

____

10. cot

____

11. sow

____

12. moth

____

LETTER PIECES

The two words have been mixed up together.

Match the letter pieces to make two words that match the pictures.

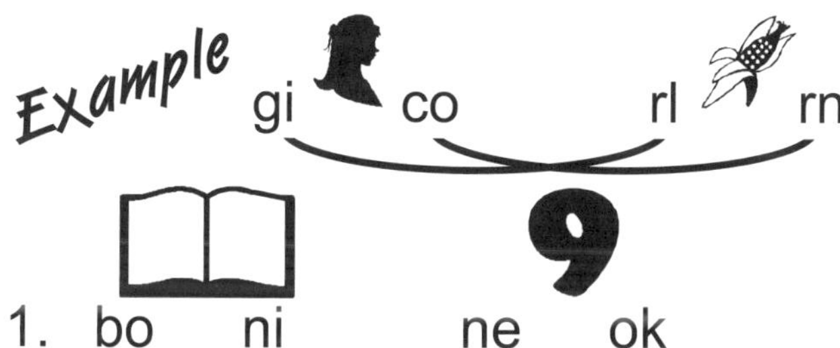

The two words are **girl** and **corn**.

1. bo ni ne ok

__________ __________

2. be mo ar on

__________ __________

3. ri dr ng um

__________ __________

4. sh ne st ip

__________ __________

5. bo st ne ar

__________ __________

6. ba bi rd by

__________ __________

7. du sh ck ed

__________ __________

8. ca ca rd ke

__________ __________

9. ga se ed te

__________ __________

10. do bu or sh

__________ __________

11. ha sh ir oe

__________ __________

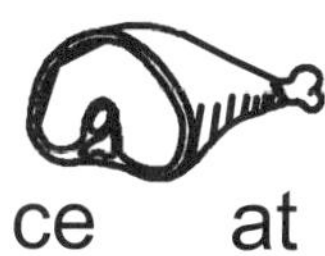

12. ra me ce at

__________ __________

SYLLABLES

A syllable contains one sounded vowel only.

Put the syllables in order to make the word suggested by the definition.

1. ga roo kan
(Australian animal)

____

2. day i hol
(a day off school)

____

3. ber De cem
(twelfth month)

____

4. el phant e
(large animal)

____

5. skel e ton
(bones of the body)

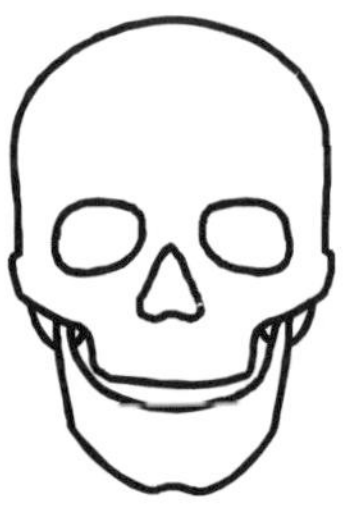

____

6. cal dar en
(a list of dates)

____

7. on ade lem
(a fizzy drink)

____

8. ter yes day
(day before today)

____

9. i an mal
(a living creature)

____

10. di no saur
(large animal that once lived on the earth)

____

SILENT LETTERS

Each of the words in the box contains a silent letter. Write each word in its correct space in the sentences. Circle the silent letters.

ghost	calf	write	knife	knee
climb	lamb	castle	whole	wrap

1. I watched the monkey

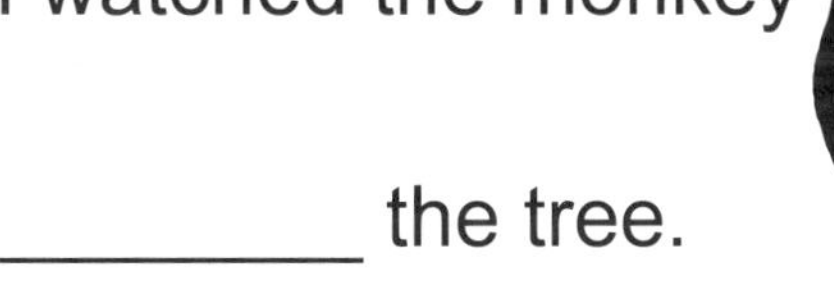

________ the tree.

2. A baby sheep is

called a ________.

3. The greedy girl ate

the ________ cake.

4. Mika slipped and

hurt her ________.

5. Some people believe a

________ lives in the haunted house.

6. The King lives in

a __________.

7. A baby cow is

called a ________.

8. I am going to ________

a story about dinosaurs.

9. Will you help me

________ the parcel up?

10. We cut the meat

with a sharp ________.

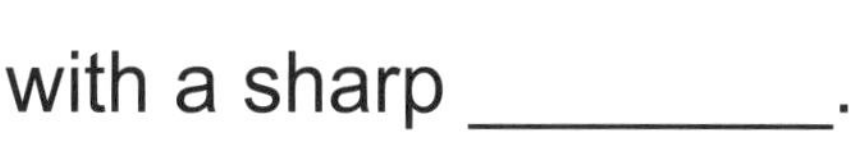

PLURAL WORDS

For most words, we add **s** to make them mean more than one.

Example dog dog**s**, boy boy**s**

Words that end in **s**, **ss**, **ch** or **sh** add **es** to mean more than one.

Example one bush two bush**es**

Write the word in brackets so it means more than one.

1. There were six ________ in the tree. (bird)
2. I ate four ________ for lunch. (apple)
3. I read two ________ last night. (book)
4. There are lots of ________ in the paddock. (cow)
5. I have two ________ in my pocket. (key)
6. I took the five ________ into the next room. (tray)
7. The children have lots of ________. (toy)
8. There were three ________ in the paddock. (donkey)
9. All the ________ broke when I dropped them. (glass)
10. My mother has two ________. (watch)
11. There are lots of ________ in our garden. (bush)
12. The children all travel to school on ________. (bus)

SPELLING RULES (1)

When we add **ed** to a word that ends in 1 vowel + 1 consonant we double the consonant.

Example pl**a** **n** pla**nn**ed

Add ed to the word in brackets and complete each sentence.

1. I ___________ the glasses on to the floor. (drop)
2. The car ___________ at the corner. (stop)
3. The dog ___________ the bone across the yard. (drag)
4. I ___________ my hands together. (rub)
5. We ___________ the hole in the wall. (plug)
6. Gina ___________ over the log. (hop)
7. Peter ___________ the dirty floor. (mop)
8. Anna ___________ up all the wood. (chop)
9. The happy girl ___________ across the yard. (skip)
10. I ___________ the window with my knuckles. (tap)

SPELLING RULES (2)

When we add **ing** to a word that ends in 1 vowel + 1 consonant we double the consonant.

Example h**o** **p** ho**pp**ing

Add ing to the word in brackets and complete each sentence.

1. I am going ___________ with my mother. (shop)
2. We are carefully ___________ over the flowers. (step)
3. Luke is ___________ across the pool. (swim)
4. The bees are ___________ loudly. (hum)
5. I am ___________ the rope into pieces. (cut)
6. The girls are ___________ across the lawn. (run)
7. I am ___________ a deep hole. (dig)
8. Than is ___________ on a seat. (sit)
9. The brave girl is ___________ the tiger. (pat)
10. I am ___________ a new bicycle for my birthday. (get)

COMPOUND WORDS

Compound words are made up of two or more smaller words.

Example eggcup is made up of ***egg*** + ***cup***.

Choose the correct word to complete each compound word.

1. Kelly has pig________.
   (birds tails)

2. Today is Cam's

   birth_______. (day cup)

3. In the bowl there is a

   gold_______. (drop fish)

4. My father made us some

   pan________ for tea.
   (weed cakes)

5. I found some sea_______ at

   the beach. (side weed)

6. The butter_______ had

   orange wings. (lace fly)

7. Please get me a

   flower_______ from the shed.
   (truck pot)

8. We played foot_______

   yesterday. (dog ball)

9. I saw a grass__________ on

   the leaf. (hopper tail)

10. I washed the dirty

    table_______. (fish cloth)

OPPOSITES

Words can be **opposite.** An opposite word means what the first word doesn't mean.

Example **wet** is the opposite of **dry**.

Choose the word from the box that is the opposite of the <u>underlined</u> word.

lost	short	cold	old	stop
buy	dirty	laugh	take	shut

1. My shirt is <u>clean</u> but Chan's is ________.

2. Chloe is going to <u>sell</u> a bike. ________

3. Lee is <u>tall</u> but Maya is ________.

4. Today it is <u>hot</u> but yesterday it was ________.

5. Please <u>open</u> the door. ________.

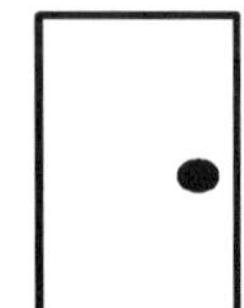

6. Tiki <u>found</u> a dollar yesterday. ________

7. When he heard the story he began to <u>cry</u>. ________

8. He likes to <u>give</u>. ________

9. Juan is <u>young</u> but Kelly is ________.

10. The car is starting to <u>go</u>. ________.

HOMOPHONES

Homophones are words that sound the same but have different spellings and different meanings.

Choose the correct homophone to fill the space. Colour it in.

1. There are

for	four

birds in the cage.

2. A rabbit has a fluffy

tail	tale

.

3. We are going

to	two

school early.

4. Did you

hear	here

what the teacher said?

5. The hot

son	sun

dried up the water.

6. I am going to

meat	meet

her tonight.

7. Last

week	weak

I won the spelling competition.

8. I helped my mother cut the

would	wood

.

9. Tony tried to

cell	sell

me his old bike.

10. I am going to

buy	by

a present for my mother.

ANAGRAMS

Anagrams are words made by rearranging the letters of another word.

Example **rat** can be rewritten as **tar**.

Rearrange the letters of the word in brackets to make a word that fits the sentence.

1. A black ________ caught a mouse. (act)
2. I fell and hurt my ________. (ram)
3. I ________ the race. (now)
4. Please turn on the ________ and get some water. (pat)
5. An ________ made its nest in our tree. (low)

6. I cut the wood with a ________. (was)
7. I like to drink hot ________. (ate)
8. I ________ an elephant at the zoo. (was)
9. Sally stuck the ________ in the balloon. (nip)
10. I washed my puppy in a ________ of water. (but)

WORDS WITH THE SAME MEANING

Some words have the same or nearly the same meaning as other words.

Example **big** means the same as **large**.

Find a word in the box that has the same meaning as the underlined word. Write it in the space at the end of the sentence.

sad	sick	close	dress	damp
yell	quickly	small	begin	nasty

1. The clothes on the line are still wet ________.
2. When will we start to pack up? ________
3. Tomi is still feeling ill. ________
4. Leah is unhappy today. ________
5. There is no need to shout. ________
6. That was a mean thing to do. ________
7. This insect is very tiny. ________
8. The park is near to our house. ________
9. He can run quite fast. ________
10. Gina wore a blue frock to school ________.

WORD MEANINGS - PLACES

Match each name in the box with the phrase which says what it is.

bridge	school	garden	zoo	airport
garage	beach	hospital	bed	store

1. a place for the care of sick people ____________
2. a place where aircraft take off ____________
3. a place to sleep ____________
4. a place for buying things ____________
5. a place for swimming and sunbaking ____________
6. a place for keeping a car ____________
7. a place to cross over water ____________
8. a place for growing plants ____________
9. a place where children learn ____________
10. a place where wild animals are kept ____________

WORD FAMILIES

Sort the words in the box into groups and write them under the correct headings.

magpie	ant	owl
grasshopper	emu	butterfly
camel	donkey	zebra

Birds	Insects	Animals
___	___	___
___	___	___
___	___	___

Sort the words in the box into groups and write them under the correct headings.

rose	carrot	yellow
orange	daisy	daffodil
beans	purple	potato

Flowers	Vegetables	Colours
___	___	___
___	___	___
___	___	___

SIMILES

To help describe something we can compare it to something else. This is called a **simile**.

Example Her hair is as **yellow as gold.**

Circle the word that best completes the simile.

1. This leaf is as green as (gold grass).
2. Alex is as busy as a (bee chair).
3. The new sheet was as white as (coal snow).
4. Our teacher is as wise as an (orange owl).
5. This meat is as hard as (cotton nails).
6. My dog is as thin as a (rake clock).
7. We think Tomi is as brave as a (bird lion).
8. These books are as light as a (car feather).
9. We all stayed as quiet as a (mouse rooster).
10. In our beds we felt as warm as (ice toast).

Write your own similes.

11. The train moved as slow as a __________.
12. She jumps as high as a __________ in sports.
13. The tissue was as soft as a __________.
14. He ran as quick as a __________.

USING A or AN BEFORE WORDS

The vowels are a, e, i, o and u.

We use **an** in front of words that begin with vowels.

Example **an** apple

We use **a** before words that begin with other letters.

Example **a** green apple

Colour the box that contains the word you should use.

1. I saw | a | an | ant.
2. Here is | a | an | egg.
3. I ate | a | an | big cake.
4. Mary has | a | an | cat.
5. Here is | a | an | bat.
6. She gave me | a | an | cap.
7. This is | a | an | fat pig.
8. We have | a | an | old car.
9. Tom kicked | a | an | ball.
10. There is | a | an | emu in the garden.

NOUNS (1)

Nouns are the names of animals or things.

Use a noun from the box to finish each nursery rhyme.

shoe	tub	hill	wall	corner

1. Rub-a-dub-dub, three men in a ______________.
2. Humpty Dumpty sat on a ______________.
3. Little Jack Horner sat in a ______________.
4. Jack and Jill went up the ______________.
5. There was an old lady who lived in a ______________.

Some nouns are the names of places people live or animals live.

Choose the noun that tells where each animal lives.

stable	shell	sty	web	nest

6. I don't know why,
   But this little pig lives in a ______________.
7. When it is able,
   A horse lives in a ______________.
8. I have heard it said,
   A spider lives in a ______________.
9. If it is feeling well,
   A snail comes out if its ______________.
10. If it needs a rest,
    A bird sits on its ______________.

NOUNS (2)

Look at the words in the box. They are all names. Read them carefully and then write them under the headings below.

shower	kettle	tree
flower	bath	stove
freezer	spade	soap

In the kitchen	In the bathroom	In the garden
____________	____________	____________
____________	____________	____________
____________	____________	____________

Draw a line from each name on the left to the name on the right. The name on the right tells what it is made of.

bottle	paper
jumper	wood
book	glass
table	wool
ball	rubber

VERBS

Verbs are words that tell us what someone or something is doing.

Circle the correct verb under each picture. Write it in the space.

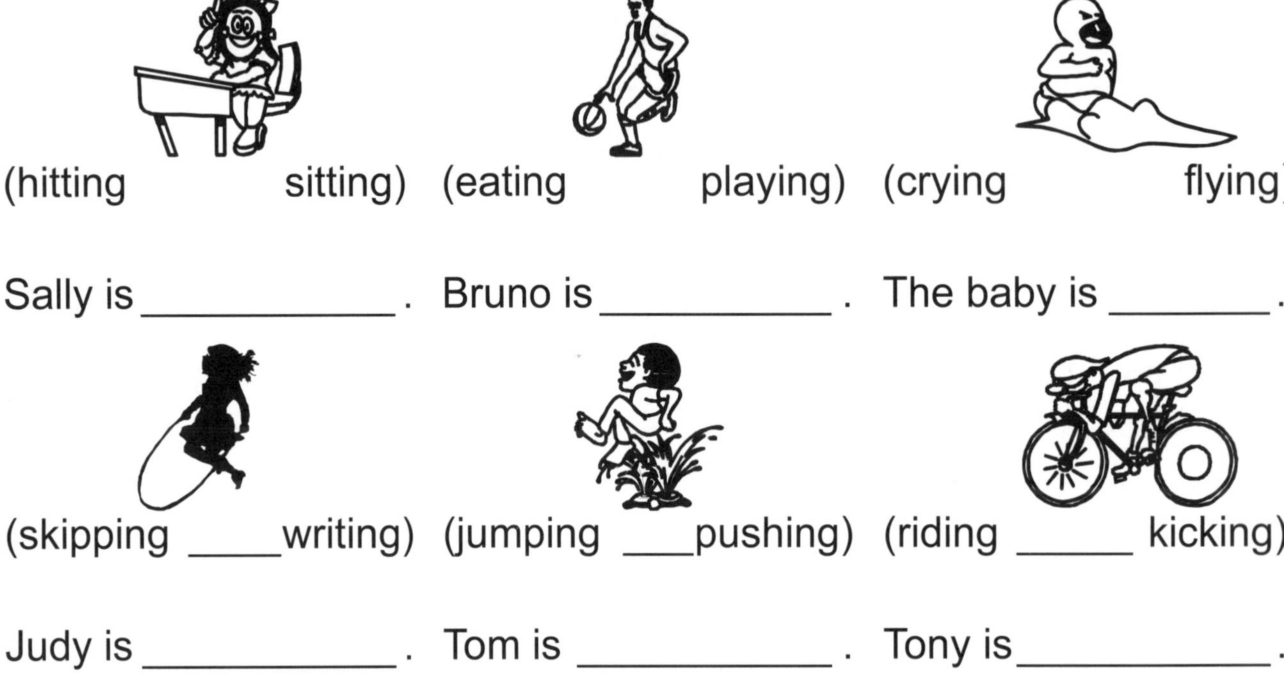

(hitting sitting) (eating playing) (crying flying)

Sally is ___________. Bruno is ___________. The baby is ________.

(skipping _____writing) (jumping ____pushing) (riding ______ kicking)

Judy is ___________. Tom is ___________. Tony is___________.

What can you do? Choose a word from the box to complete each sentence. Write the word in the space.

1. Can you ____________________ a floor?
2. Can you ____________________ a bike?
3. Can you ____________________ a kite?
4. Can you ____________________ a letter?
5. Can you ____________________ the dishes?
6. Can you ____________________ a hole?

dig
fly
post
sweep
ride
wash

VERBS - TENSE

Verbs can show something happening now. For example: I **am** playing.

Verbs can show something that has already happened.
For example: I **played** yesterday.

Verbs can show something that will happen in the future.
For example: I **will play** tomorrow.

Choose the correct verb from the box and write it in the space.

driving	playing	digging	sweeping	eating	riding

1. Mike is __________ a hole.
2. Joe is __________ a bike.
3. Chan is __________ a pie.
4. Tom is __________ the floor.
5. Sally is __________ a game.
6. Mr Smith is __________ a car.

Colour the box that contains the correct verb.

1. Mike [ate / eat] a pie for lunch.

2. Sally will [walk / walked] to school tomorrow.
3. Yesterday I [go / went] to the football.

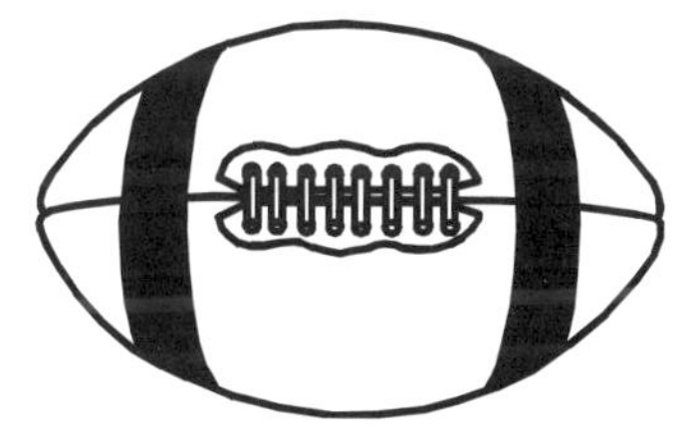

4. Jack will [win / won] the race easily.
5. This morning my pencils [fell / fall] on to the floor.
6. We will [help / helped] you tomorrow.

USING IS and ARE

We use **is** when we are talking about **one** person or thing.

We use **are** when we are talking about **two or more** people or things.

Colour the correct word.

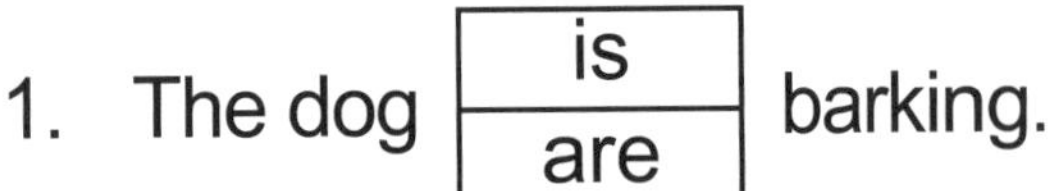

1. The dog	is / are	barking.	
2. The boys	is / are	coming.	
3. The horses	is / are	galloping.	
4. The ships	is / are	sailing.	
5. An ant	is / are	an insect.	
6. They	is / are	playing a game.	
7. These books	is / are	old.	
8. Judy	is / are	riding a bike.	

USING WAS and WERE

We use **was** when we are talking about **one** person or thing.

We use **were** when we are talking about **two or more** people or things.

Colour the correct word.

1. A bird	was / were	flying.
2. The trains	was / were	leaving.
3. Snow	was / were	falling.
4. A duck	was / were	swimming.
5. The stars	was / were	twinkling.
6. She	was / were	sweeping the floor.
7. They	was / were	in the room.
8. The gate	was / were	open.

ADJECTIVES

Adjectives are words that describe a naming word.

Example a **blue** dress a **rubber** ball

Choose the best describing word. Circle it.

1. A fire is — cold / wet / hot
2. Snow is — cold / fat / wet
3. Wool is — sweet / soft / happy
4. An elephant is — purple / round / big
5. A mouse is — purple / round / small
6. An apple is — red / silly / blue

Choose a describing word from the box to fill in the spaces.

fast	old	blue	shut	yellow	sharp

1. On a sunny day the sky is __________.
2. A ripe banana is __________.
3. If I win a race I am __________.
4. If a door is closed it is __________.
5. If I live for a long time I will be __________.
6. A knife is often very __________.

ADVERBS

Adverbs tell us how, when or where something is done.

Example

The dog barked **loudly**. *(how)*

The dog barked **yesterday**. *(when)*

The dog barked **there**. *(where)*

Read the sentences. Write the correct adverb in the space.

1. We will come __________. *(when)* (tonight here)

2. He ran very __________. *(how)* (fast later)

3. We went __________. *(where)* (inside often)

4. She stood __________. *(how)* (here still)

5. I won the race ____________. *(when)* (yesterday hard)

6. He lost his pen __________. *(where)* (later here)

7. Tom will come __________. *(when)* (soon softly)

8. Snails move __________. *(how)* (tomorrow slowly)

9. We are playing football __________. *(when)* (there today)

10. The baby cried __________. *(how)* (sadly then)

PREPOSITIONS

Prepositions tell us the position of people or things.

Look at the picture and then circle the correct word below.

1. A snake is climbing ___________ the tree. (up under)
2. A lizard is sitting ___________ a rock. (over on)
3. A boy is hiding ___________ a tree. (above behind)
4. A girl is jumping ___________ the tree. (off beside)
5. A kangaroo is ___________ the rocks. (above between)
6. A dog is jumping ___________ the bush. (over under)
7. The sun is shining ___________ the tree. (above under)

PRONOUNS

A pronoun is a word used instead of a noun.

Example **Jack** went out. **He** went out. **<u>He</u>** is a pronoun.

Read the sentences. Choose the correct pronoun to fill the space.

1. (He They)
   One day Tom's father came home from work.

   ______ had some coins in his pocket.

   ______ were very shiny.

2. (They her)
   Sally's mother went to the supermarket.

   Sally went with ______ .

   ______ bought some lollies.

3. (It He)
   Tim spoke to the puppy.

   ______ was eating a bone.

   ______ patted the puppy.

4. (They her)
   The boys met Sally.

   ______ gave ______ some apples.

5. (She her)
   Yesterday Sally made a cake.

   ______ mixed flour and water together.

   I helped ______ eat the cakes.

6. (me She)
   I was not working. The teacher was angry.

   ______ took the pencil from

   ______ .

7. (them They)
   I found the dog the boys had lost.

   ______ were very happy when

   I gave it back to ______ .

8. (ours you)
   This cat belongs to our family.

   This cat is ______ . It does

   not belong to ______ .

CONJUNCTIONS

Conjunctions are words used to join words or sentences together.

Example bat **and** ball

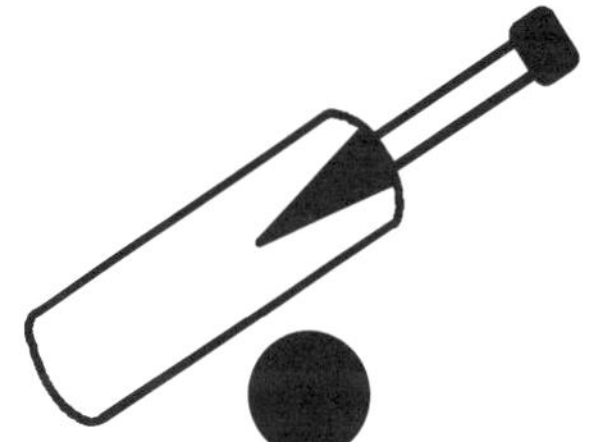

Add the correct conjunction in the space.

1. I washed the dishes ________ Mike dried them.
   (and for)

2. I will not help you ________ you try harder.
   (unless who)

3. We will get wet ________ it rains.
   (for if)

4. We must wait here ________ the rain stops.
   (until which)

5. I could not come ____________ I was sick.
   (because that)

6. I have not seen Molly ________ last week.
   (since yet)

7. Jo got into trouble ________ being naughty.
   (for until)

8. I did not know ________ stole my pencils.
   (who until)

9. Mike is big ________ he is very gentle.
   (but which)

10. I saw the dog ________ stole the meat.
    (yet that)

PHRASES

A phrase is a group of words. It can tell us where or when something happened.

Example I played **last night**. *(when)* I played **in the park**. *(where)*

Read the sentences. Write the correct phrase to finish the sentence.

1. Mike was ten years old

   ______________________.

   (last Tuesday, in the kettle)

2. The dog is

   ______________________.

   (in the kennel, at six o'clock)

3. We played football

   ______________________.

   (in the park, in the oven)

4. We sleep

   ______________________.

   (up the tree, in a bed)

5. School begins

   ______________________.

   (at nine o'clock, at six o'clock)

6. I saw the dog

   ______________________.

   (with the long tail, with glasses)

7. The snake crawled

   ______________________.

   (under the rock, with big ears)

8. I spoke to the man

   ______________________.

   (with eight legs, with the long beard)

9. I caught the train

   ______________________.

   (at the station, in the kitchen)

10. We left school

    ______________________.

    (at four o'clock, with big ears)

SENTENCES

A sentence is a group of words that make **sense**.
They always have a verb (doing word).

Circle the ending that best completes each sentence. Draw pictures for the groups of words that don't make sense.

1. Tim was crying
   a) because he was sad.
   b) because he was asleep.

2. A black cat
   a) chased a mouse.
   b) on the rocks.

3. A small bird
   a) with four legs.
   b) flew over my head.

4. We must stay here
   a) until the rain stops.
   b) began to growl.

5. I cooked the cakes
   a) with big legs.
   b) and Mike ate them.

6. A flower
   a) has lots of petals.
   b) has four legs.

7. Joanne can't come to school
   a) because she is too young.
   b) over the moon.

8. We use pencils
   a) to draw.
   b) to eat.

9. I can tie
   a) my shoelaces.
   b) has an engine.

10. A pig
    a) has four legs.
    b) can fly.

STATEMENTS

A sentence begins with a capital letter and ends with a full stop.

Example It is cold.

Rewrite each sentence with a capital letter and a full stop.

1. the dog is in the car

____

____

2. that is a big tree

____

____

3. it is nearly time to go

____

____

4. he is in the room

____

____

5. she is playing a game

____

____

6. my cat is called Fluffy

____

____

7. my father did the dishes

____

____

8. i put the cup on the bench

____

____

9. this is an old table

____

____

10. go to your room now

____

____

QUESTIONS

A question begins with a capital letter and ends with a question mark.

Example **W**hat is your name**?**

Write each question with a capital letter and a question mark.

1. what time is it

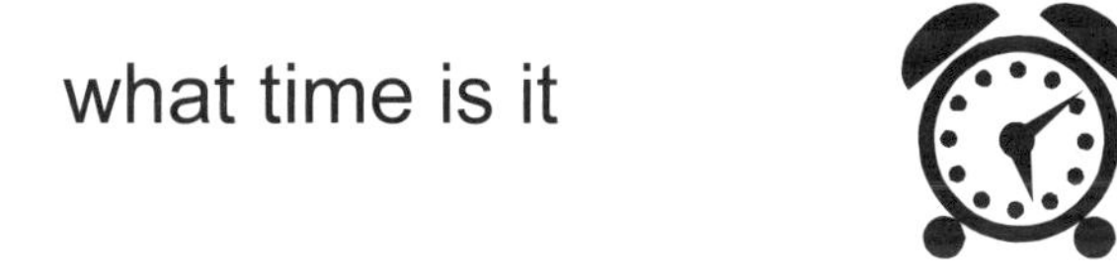

2. where is our teacher

3. where is the pencil you borrowed

4. when will he get here

5. does Jared play tennis

6. how did Elly get here so early

7. why did you do that

8. what type of animal is a horse

9. when will it be lunchtime

10. why are you climbing the tree

11. do you like eating pizza

12. is Tai your sister

STATEMENTS AND QUESTIONS

There are different types of sentences.
A **statement** begins with a capital letter and ends with a full stop.

Example My name is Peter.

A **question** begins with a capital letter and ends with a question mark.

Example What is your name?

Circle the sentence in each pair that has correct punctuation. Write the other sentence with correct punctuation.

1. Where did David go?
   it is getting cold.

   ____

2. I haven't seen Matthew today.
   the old man rode a bicycle.

   ____

3. This tree has brown leaves
   I put the book on the table.

   ____

4. Do you like apples.
   The dog is in a kennel.

   ____

5. Does your mother drive a car?
   Where is your new bike

   ____

6. where has Sally gone?
   My best friend is Paul.

   ____

7. they are jumping over the rope.
   He is sitting on the seat.

   ____

8. who stole the diamonds?
   What day is it today?

   ____

9. A rose is a flower
   A pig is an animal.

   ____

10. my favourite food is pizza.
    What time is it?

    ____

STATEMENTS, QUESTIONS AND EXCLAMATIONS

There are different types of sentences.

A **statement** sentence ends with a full stop.

A **question** sentence ends with a question mark.

An **exclamation** sentence is a sentence that expresses a strong emotion. It ends with an exclamation mark (!). Exclamation sentences are often short.

Example Stop! What a beautiful baby!

Write each sentence with the correct punctuation mark.

1. Our school has ten teachers

   ____

   ____

2. What a lovely day

   ____

   ____

3. Look out

   ____

   ____

4. Where did you get the pie

   ____

   ____

5. Why did you call Sam

   ____

   ____

6. How terrible

   ____

   ____

7. What time are we leaving

   ____

   ____

8. I caught three fish yesterday

   ____

   ____

9. This is an interesting book

   ____

   ____

10. When did the bell ring

    ____

    ____

COMMAS

Commas are used to separate words in a list.

Example I own a pony, a dog, a cat and a goldfish.

Write the sentences with commas.

1. My best friends are Terri Elsa Bruno and Sadiki.

2. The colours on the flag are red blue green and yellow.

3. I like to eat apples pears bananas and apricots.

4. Bees ants butterflies and wasps are all types of insect.

5. A carpenter uses a hammer nails a saw and a chisel.

6. Lin likes to play soccer tennis netball and cricket.

7. In my desk there are pens pencils books and erasers.

8. Magpies ducks geese and swans are all types of birds.